AF897709

Media Law in Croatia

Media Law in Croatia

Hrvoje Lisičar
Marko Turudić

This book was originally published as a monograph in the International Encyclopaedia of Laws/Media Law.

Founding Editor: Roger Blanpain
General Editor: Frank Hendrickx
Volume Editors: Peggy Valcke & Eva Lievens

Wolters Kluwer

Published by:
Kluwer Law International B.V.
PO Box 316
2400 AH Alphen aan den Rijn
The Netherlands
E-mail: international-sales@wolterskluwer.com
Website: lrus.wolterskluwer.com

Sold and distributed in North, Central and South America by:
Wolters Kluwer Legal & Regulatory U.S.
7201 McKinney Circle
Frederick, MD 21704
United States of America
Email: customer.service@wolterskluwer.com

Sold and distributed in all other countries by:
Air Business Subscriptions
Rockwood House
Haywards Heath
West Sussex
RH16 3DH
United Kingdom
Email: international-customerservice@wolterskluwer.com

DISCLAIMER: The material in this volume is in the nature of general comment only. It is not offered as advice on any particular matter and should not be taken as such. The editor and the contributing authors expressly disclaim all liability to any person with regard to anything done or omitted to be done, and with respect to the consequences of anything done or omitted to be done wholly or partly in reliance upon the whole or any part of the contents of this volume. No reader should act or refrain from acting on the basis of any matter contained in this volume without first obtaining professional advice regarding the particular facts and circumstances at issue. Any and all opinions expressed herein are those of the particular author and are not necessarily those of the editor or publisher of this volume.

Printed on acid-free paper

ISBN 978-94-035-0781-1

e-Book: ISBN 978-94-035-0782-8
web-PDF: ISBN 978-94-035-0783-5

© 2019, Kluwer Law International BV, The Netherlands

All rights reserved. No part of this publication may be reproduced, stored in a retrieval system, or transmitted in any form or by any means, electronic, mechanical, photocopying, recording, or otherwise, without the prior written permission of the publisher.

Permission to use this content must be obtained from the copyright owner. More information can be found at: lrus.wolterskluwer.com/policies/permissions-reprints-and-licensing

Printed in the United Kingdom.

The Authors

Hrvoje Lisičar is an assistant professor of Law at the Faculty of Law, University of Zagreb. He received his PhD in 2012, for his doctoral thesis on 'The Influence of High Technologies on Legal Regulation of Electronic Media'. Hrvoje teaches several courses at the Faculty of Law, University of Zagreb, including Electronic Media Law, Information Technology Law, Internet Governance and Regulation, Electronic Media Law, Cybercrime and Cybersecurity, Introduction to Information Security and Privacy and Electronic Communications. He is also a lecturer for the postgraduate programme in Rights of Children (course – Media and Children) organized by the Faculty of Law, University of Zagreb. His academic research focuses on the regulation of electronic media, Internet governance, data protection and information law and policy affecting the flow of information in digital society. Hrvoje is the author and co-author of numerous publications on the regulation of electronic media, data protection, self -regulation and co-regulation in online media. As a member of numerous working groups, he was involved in the process of drafting national strategies and laws that regulate information security and online media in Croatia. He is a member of the Croatian Academy of Legal Science.

Marko Turudić is an assistant professor at the University of Zagreb Law School. He graduated from the University of Zagreb Law School in July 2007. Immediately after graduation, he started working as a junior associate at *Laktić and Partners Law Firm* and, in 2008, he started working as an assistant at the Study Centre for Public Administration and Public Finances in Zagreb. In November 2009, he started working as an assistant at the Department of Administrative Law, University of Zagreb Law School. His research interests include regulation of network industries (in particular, electronic communications) and public procurement. He teaches at the University of Zagreb Law School, Study Centre for Public Administration and Public Finances in Zagreb and the Social Work Study Centre. He is a visiting lecturer at the International Christian University (Tokyo, Japan: EU Administrative Law and EU Electronic Communications Regulation), China University of Political Science and Law (Beijing, China: EU Administrative Law, EU Electronic Communications Regulation) and the Double Degree Programme in Intellectual Property Law offered by the Ss. Cyril and Methodius University and the University of Strasbourg (EU Electronic Communications Regulation). He is a full member of the Croatian Academy of Legal Science. For the list of his published papers. *See*: http://www.pravo.unizg.hr/en/marko.turudic.

Acknowledgements

The authors would like to extend their gratitude to Assistant Professor Marko Jurić, Faculty of Law, University of Zagreb, Croatia for his help and contribution in writing several chapters of this monograph.

Acknowledgements

Table of Contents

List of Abbreviations

ADA	Administrative Disputes Act
AIA	Access to Information Act
APC	Agency for Protection of Competition
AVMSD	Audiovisual Media Services Directive
BiH	Bosnia and Herzegovina
CA	Courts Act
CC	Criminal Code
CJA	The Croatian Journalists' Association
CNBA	The Croatian National Bank Act
COA	Civil Obligations Act
Council of HRT	Programme Council of HRT
COPA	Competition Protection Act
CPA	Civil Procedure Act
CPC	Criminal Procedure Code
CRTA	Croatian Radio-Television Act
ECA	Electronic Communications Act
EMA	Electronic Media Act
EMC	Electronic Media Council of the Republic of Croatia
EU	European Union
HAKOM	Croatian Electronic Communications and Rail Regulatory agency
HAVC	Croatian Audiovisual Centre
HRT	Croatian Radio-Television
MA	Media Act
MDA	Misdemeanour Act
OPM	Ordinance on the Protection of Minors in Electronic Media
PIPA	Personal Information Protection Act
RERC	Rules for the exercise of the right to correction in programmes of audio and audiovisual media service providers

List of Abbreviations

SAA	State Attorney's Act
SFRY	Socialist Federative Republic of Yugoslavia
TUCJ	Trade Union of the Croatian Journalists

General Introduction

§1. General Background of the Country

I. Political and Legal System of the Country

A. *The Transition from Communism to Democracy*

1. The Republic of Croatia has been a democratic country only for the past twenty-five years. The transition from communism to democracy began in the late eighties and early nineties of the twentieth century, with the dissolution of the Socialist Federal Republic of Yugoslavia (SFRY). The common understanding is that the process of disintegration of Yugoslavia began with the death of Josip Broz Tito on 4 May 1980. He was one of the creators and the driving and unifying force of the former State and the person whose (almost) unquestionable authority held opposing interests of all the people of Yugoslavia under control. Shortly after the death of Josip Broz Tito, there was another important factor that significantly contributed to the breakup of Yugoslavia: the economic crisis. Croatia, at the time, recorded a new wave of political arrests and persecution of Croatian open-minded intellectuals, and relations in Kosovo were radically changing, which threatened all-out war, with international implications. One of the most important and most direct causes of the necessary disintegration of the country was a new wave of Serbian nationalism, which was no longer covert and very openly expressed.[1]

2. This situation culminated in the elections for the Parliament (*Sabor*) of the Socialist Republic of Croatia,[2] which took place in two rounds, on 22 April and 6 May 1990. The Croatian Democratic Union (HDZ) led by Franjo Tuđman won the elections, with a firm commitment towards independence and democratic change. In these elections, the Social Democratic Party of Croatia (SDP, the successor of the Croatian Communist Party (SKH, League of Communists of Croatia) when it merged with its parallel Social Democratic Party of Croatia (SDSH)) became the main opposition party. The Croatian Parliament was constituted on 30 May 1990. It can be said that with this date the formal creation of the Republic of Croatia began.

1. Fabijanić Gagro, S., Vukas, B., *Pravna priroda i politička pozadina oružanih sukoba u Hrvatskoj i Bosni i Hercegovini* [Legal Nature and Political Background of Armed Conflicts in Croatia and Bosnia and Herzegovina], *Zbornik Pravnog fakulteta Sveučilišta u Zagrebu* [University of Zagreb Law School Collected Papers] 58 (5) 1159–2000 (2008): 1166.
2. The Socialist Republic of Croatia was one of the six federal states of SFRY.

Shortly thereafter, on 17 August 1990, began an armed rebellion of Croatian Serbs, which would be a prelude for the future direct aggression of the JNA and Serbian forces (JNA) from Serbia. It is necessary to observe the whole process of acquiring Croatian independence through this context.

3. In December 1990, Parliament adopted the Croatian Constitution (so-called Christmas Constitution), which forms an integral whole with the constitutional decision of 25 June 1991 and those from 8 October 1991, and despite its three amendments (of 1997 and the so-called amendments to the Constitution of 2000 and 2001) this Constitution, up to the present day, forms the foundation of the modern Croatian State. The new Constitution proclaims the universal democratic principles, human rights and the protection of minorities.

4. Not even six months after the adoption of the new Constitution, the president of the Republic of Croatia adopted a 'Decision' to call for an independence referendum on 25 April 1991, which was held on 19 May 1991. The referendum offered two options; the questions were the following: '(1) Are you in favour of the Republic of Croatia, as a sovereign and independent State, which guarantees cultural autonomy and all civil rights to Serbs and members of other nationalities in Croatia, and can enter into a union of sovereign States with other republics (as proposed by Croatia and Slovenia for the solution of the Yugoslavia crisis)? and (2) Are you in favour of the Republic of Croatia to remain in Yugoslavia as a single federal State (according to the proposal of the Republic of Serbia and the Socialist Republic of Montenegro for the solution of the Yugoslavia crisis)?' Over 90% of Croatian citizens (93.24%) voted for the first question, i.e., for the independence of the Republic of Croatia.

5. At the session of 25 June 1991, the Parliament adopted important constitutional Acts with which an independent and sovereign Republic of Croatia was declared. These were the 'Constitutional Decision on Sovereignty and Independence of the Republic of Croatia' and the 'Declaration on the Sovereignty and Independence of the Republic of Croatia'.

6. Shortly after the successful referendum on independence and the secession from Yugoslavia, there was a significant escalation of hostilities. The JNA attacked Slovenia immediately after Slovenia's declaration of independence, and the war in Croatia escalated into an open aggression of Serbia and Montenegro (assisted by the JNA). Shortly thereafter, the war in Bosnia and Herzegovina (BiH) began.

7. Shortly after the declaration of independence the first wave of recognition of the Croatian independence began to arrive, while the largest and most important wave came in 1992. The war lasted until 1995 when the successful military action of the Croatian armed forces 'Operation Storm' liberated one-third of Croatian territory, which indirectly led to the Dayton Accords.

B. Republic of Croatia: Overview

8. Today, Croatia is a unitary democratic republic. The Republic of Croatia has consistently implemented the division of power in the executive, legislative and judicial branches. Executive power is divided between the government and the president, with the president's powers largely ceremonial (with the exception of foreign affairs and defence). The Republic of Croatia is a member of the United Nations, the World Trade Organization, the Mediterranean Union, NATO and, from 1 July 2013, the European Union (EU).

1. Parliament

9. The Croatian Parliament is called *Sabor*. The structure, powers and elections to *Sabor* are regulated by the Constitution of the Republic of Croatia[3] (the Constitution), the Rules of Procedure of *Sabor*[4] and the Act on the election of Members of *Sabor*.[5] *Sabor* is a representative body of the citizens and the legislative body of the Republic of Croatia and has at least 100 and no more than 160 members, on the basis of universal and equal suffrage, by direct secret ballot.[6] Representatives are elected for a term of four years.

10. Members of *Sabor* shall enjoy immunity. A representative may be detained without the approval of *Sabor* only if he/she is caught in the criminal offence for which a punishment of imprisonment of more than five years is prescribed. In such a case, the Speaker of *Sabor* shall be informed. If *Sabor* is not in session, authorization to arrest the representative, or to continue criminal proceedings, and his possible right to immunity is decided by the Mandate and Immunity Committee, whose decision is subject to subsequent confirmation by *Sabor*.[7]

11. *Sabor* decides on the enactment and amendment of the Constitution, passes laws, adopts the State budget, decides on war and peace, passes Acts which express the policy of *Sabor*, passes the Strategy of National Security and Strategy of the Croatian Defence, exercises civil control over the armed forces and security services of Croatia, decides on amending the Croatian borders, calls referendums, carries out elections, appointments and reliefs, in accordance with the Constitution and law, supervises the work of the Croatian government and other holders of public office responsible to *Sabor*, in accordance with the Constitution and law, grants amnesty for criminal offences and performs other tasks stipulated by the Constitution.[8]

3. The Constitution of the Republic of Croatia, Official Gazette [OG] No. 56/90, 135/97, 8/98, 113/00, 124/00, 28/01, 41/01, 55/01, 76/10, 85/10, 05/14.
4. Rules of Procedure of *Sabor*, Official Gazette [OG] No. 81/13.
5. Act on election of Members of *Sabor*, Official Gazette [OG] No. 116/99, 109/00, 53/03, 69/03, 167/03, 44/06, 19/07, 20/09, 145/10, 24/11, 93/11, 120/11, 19/15.
6. Article 72 of the Constitution.
7. Article 75 of the Constitution.
8. Article 80 of the Constitution.

12. If the Constitution does not provide otherwise, *Sabor* shall make decisions by majority vote if the session is attended by a majority of the Members of Parliament. Laws (organic laws) regulating the rights of national minorities shall be adopted by a two-thirds majority vote of all representatives. *Sabor* shall adopt laws (organic laws) which elaborate the constitutionally defined human rights and fundamental freedoms, the electoral system, the organization, jurisdiction and operation of government bodies and the organization and authority of local and regional governments, by a majority vote of all the members.[9]

13. *Sabor* may, for a maximum period of one year, authorize the Croatian government to regulate, by decrees, certain issues within its competence, except those relating to the elaboration of the constitutionally defined human rights and fundamental freedoms, national rights, the electoral system, the organization, jurisdiction and of government bodies and local self-governments. Decrees based on statutory authority shall not have retroactive effect. The regulation adopted on the basis of statutory authority shall cease to apply upon expiry of a period of one year from the date of the receipt of authority to adopt them unless *Sabor* decides otherwise.[10]

2. Government

14. The Croatian government is the main executive body of the Republic of Croatia and exercises its executive power in accordance with the Constitution and laws. It is composed of the president, one or more vice presidents and ministers. Without the approval of the government, the president and members of the government may not perform any other public or professional duties.[11] Members of the government are proposed by the person to whom the President of the Republic entrusted the mandate to form the government. Immediately after the assembly of the government, and at the latest within thirty days of acceptance of the mandate, the mandatary is required to present the programme and seek a vote of confidence.[12] The government takes office when it is approved by the majority of all the Members of *Sabor*. The president and members of the government shall take a solemn oath before the Croatian Parliament. The text of the oath shall be established by law. Based on the decision of the Croatian Parliament, which expressed confidence in the Croatian government, a decision on the appointment of the prime minister is issued by the president and countersigned by the 'President of *Sabor*', and the decision on the appointment of members of the government is issued by the prime minister and countersigned by the President of *Sabor*.

15. The Croatian government proposes laws and other Acts to *Sabor*, proposes the State budget and final accounts, enforces laws and other decisions of *Sabor*, passes regulations for the implementation of the law, conducts foreign and internal

9. Article 83 of the Constitution.
10. Article 88 of the Constitution.
11. Article 108 of the Constitution.
12. Article 109 of the Constitution.

politics, directs and supervises the work of the State administration responsible for the economic development of the country, directs the operation and development of public services, performs other duties specified by the Constitution and the law.[13] The government is responsible to *Sabor;* the president and members of the government shall be jointly responsible for the decisions made by the government and individually responsible for their area of work.[14]

16. The Constitution specifically regulates the process of addressing the procedure for a vote of no confidence to the government. On the proposal of at least one-fifth of the representatives of *Sabor*, a vote of no confidence against the prime minister, an individual government member or the government as a whole can be started. A vote of no confidence against the government may be requested by its president. No discussion or vote on the no-confidence petition may be started before the lapse of seven days from the date of submission of the proposal to *Sabor*. The debate and the vote of no confidence must be carried out no later than thirty days from the date of submission of the proposal to *Sabor*. The decision of no confidence is successful if it has been voted for by the majority of the total number of representatives in *Sabor*. If *Sabor* rejects the no-confidence motion, representatives who presented it may not resubmit the same proposal before the expiry of six months. If a vote of no confidence against the prime minister, or the government as a whole, passes, the prime minister and the government shall resign. If there is no vote of confidence within thirty days for the president-elect and his or her government, the President of *Sabor* shall notify the president. After receiving the notice of the President of *Sabor*, the president will immediately take a decision to dissolve the Parliament and simultaneously call elections for *Sabor*. If a vote of no confidence is issued for an individual member of the government, the prime minister may, instead, propose another member to *Sabor*, to give him or her a vote of confidence, or the prime minister and the government may resign.[15]

3. The President

17. Croatia has, since its independence, until the end of the 1990s, had a presidential system of executive power in which the president has more executive powers than the government. Constitutional amendments introduced a semi-presidential system, which significantly limited presidential powers, and the president has become a largely ceremonial function, with specific powers in the regulation of foreign affairs and defence. The Croatian president represents the Republic of Croatia at home and abroad, ensures regular and harmonized functioning and stability of the State government and is responsible for the defence of the independence and territorial integrity of the Republic of Croatia.[16]

---

13. Article 110 of the Constitution.
14. Article 112 of the Constitution.
15. Article 113 of the Constitution.
16. Article 94 of the Constitution.

18. The president is elected by universal and equal suffrage at direct elections by secret ballot for a term of five years. One person can serve a maximum of two presidential terms. President is elected by a majority of all voters who voted. If none of the candidates obtained such a majority, a new election shall be held after fourteen days. At the new election, the right to be elected is acquired by the two candidates who received the most votes in the first round. If one of the candidates withdraws, the right to be elected is acquired by the candidate who is next in the number of votes obtained. Election of the president shall be held at least thirty, and no more than sixty, days before the expiry of the mandate of the current president. Before taking office, the president shall take a solemn oath on the Constitution before the 'President of the Croatian Constitutional Court'. The election, the oath and its recitation shall be regulated by law.[17]

19. In the case of a short absence due to illness or annual leave, the president can entrust the President of *Sabor* to replace him. In the case of a long absence due to illness or disability, especially if the president is unable to decide on entrusting the duties to a temporary substitute, the President of *Sabor* takes over as interim president based on the decision of the Constitutional Court, on the proposal of the government. In case of death, resignation or when the Constitutional Court determines the reasons for the termination of the mandate of the president, the duty of the temporary president by virtue of the Constitution is assigned to the President of *Sabor*. When the President of *Sabor*, while serving as interim president, passes an Act on the promulgation of a law, the Act must be co-signed by the president of the Croatian government. Elections for the new president must be held within sixty days of taking the office by the interim president.[18]

20. The president calls for the elections for *Sabor* and convenes its first session, calls for referendums, gives the mandate to form the government to the person who enjoys the confidence of the majority of all the representatives upon the distribution of seats in *Sabor* and according to consultations. The president also grants pardons, confers decorations and awards specified by law and performs other duties specified by the Constitution.[19] The president and the Croatian government cooperate in the formulation and execution of foreign policy. The president, on the proposal of the government and with the countersignature of the prime minister, decides on the establishment of diplomatic missions and consular offices. The president, on the proposal of the government and with the opinion of the authorized committee of *Sabor*, decides on the appointment and recall of heads of diplomatic missions, with prior countersignature of the prime minister. He also receives the credentials and letters of recall of foreign diplomatic representatives.[20]

21. The president is the supreme commander of the Croatian armed forces. He or she appoints and dismisses military commanders, in accordance with the law.

17. Article 95 of the Constitution.
18. Article 97 of the Constitution.
19. Article 98 of the Constitution.
20. Article 98 of the Constitution.

Based on the decision of *Sabor*, the president may declare war and conclude peace. In the case of an immediate threat to the independence, unity and existence of the State the president may, with the countersignature of the prime minister, make use of the armed forces, although a state of war was not declared.[21] During a state of war, the president may issue decrees with the force of law on the basis of and within the authority obtained from *Sabor*. If *Sabor* is not in session, the president has the power to issue decrees with the force of laws to regulate all the issues required by the state of war. In the case of an immediate threat to the independence, unity and existence of the State, or when government bodies are prevented from regularly performing their constitutional duties, the president may, on the recommendation of the prime minister and with his or her countersignature, issue decrees with the force of law. The President of the Republic shall submit decrees with the force of law for approval to *Sabor* as soon as *Sabor* can assemble. If the president does not submit a decree to *Sabor* for confirmation, or if *Sabor* fails to approve a decree with the force of law, it ceases to be valid.[22]

4. Constitutional Court

22. The Constitutional Court can legitimately be considered as the 'fourth branch of government' of Croatia. Although Croatia has a long tradition of constitutional adjudication, which reaches up to Yugoslavia, only with the democratic changes, the Constitutional Court acquired the possibility of complete independent action. The Croatian Constitutional Court consists of thirteen judges elected by *Sabor* by a two-thirds majority vote of all representatives from among eminent lawyers, especially judges, public prosecutors, lawyers and university professors of law, in the manner and in the procedure prescribed by constitutional law. The mandate of the judges of the Constitutional Court lasts eight years and shall be extended until the entry into office of a new judge when at its expiry this new judge has not yet been elected or has not taken office, but for no longer than six months. The process of nomination of judges to the Constitutional Court and the proposal for *Sabor* is conducted by *Sabor*'s Constitutional Committee. The President of the Constitutional Court shall be elected from among the Court's members for a four-year term.[23] The judges of the Constitutional Court may not perform any other public or professional duty. Judges of the Croatian Constitutional Court enjoy the same immunity as representatives of *Sabor*. A judge of the Constitutional Court may be dismissed before the expiry of his term if he or she asks to be relieved, if he/she is sentenced to prison or if he/she is permanently, as established by the Court, incapable of performing his/her duties.[24]

23. The Croatian Constitutional Court: decides on the constitutionality of a law; decides on the conformity of other regulations with the Constitution and law; may

21. Article 100 of the Constitution.
22. Article 100 of the Constitution.
23. Article 122 of the Constitution.
24. Article 124 of the Constitution.

review the constitutionality of laws and the constitutionality and legality of other regulations that have expired if, from this termination to the request or proposal to initiate proceedings, more than one year has passed; decides on constitutional complaints against the individual decisions of governmental bodies, local (regional) government and legal entities with public authority, when these decisions violate human rights and fundamental freedoms and the right to local and regional self-government guaranteed by the Constitution; monitors the realization of constitutionality and legality and the instances of unconstitutionality and illegality of *Sabor*; resolves jurisdictional disputes between the legislative, executive and judicial bodies; decides, in accordance with the Constitution, on the impeachment of the president; supervises the constitutionality of the programmes and activities of political parties and may, in accordance with the Constitution, ban their work; supervises the constitutionality and legality of elections and national referenda; and decides on electoral disputes which are not within the jurisdiction of courts; as well as perform other duties specified by the Constitution.[25]

24. If the Constitutional Court finds that the competent body has not passed a regulation to execute provisions of the Constitution, laws and other regulations while it was obliged to pass such a regulation, the Constitutional Court shall notify the government, and, about the regulations that were required to be adopted by the government, *Sabor*.[26] The Constitutional Court shall repeal a law if it finds it to be unconstitutional. The Constitutional Court shall repeal or annul any other regulation if it finds it to be unconstitutional or illegal.[27] The constitutional law on the Constitutional Court regulates the procedure and conditions for the election of judges of the Constitutional Court and the termination of their duties, terms and conditions for the initiation of proceedings to review constitutionality and legality, procedure and legal effects of its decisions, protection of human rights and fundamental freedoms guaranteed by the Constitution and other issues important for the performance of duties and functions of the Constitutional Court.

5. Local and Regional Government

25. The Croatian Constitution guarantees its citizens the right to a local and regional government. The right to self-government is realized through local or regional representative bodies, composed of members elected in free elections by secret ballot on the basis of direct, equal and universal suffrage. Citizens may directly participate in the management of local affairs through meetings, referenda and other forms of direct decision-making in accordance with law and statute. The rights referred to in this article in Croatia are also available to the citizens of the EU, in accordance with law and the *acquis communautaire*.[28]

25. Article 125 of the Constitution.
26. Article 125a of the Constitution.
27. Article 126 of the Constitution.
28. Article 128 of the Constitution.

26. Local government units are municipalities and towns. District (regional) self-government units are counties. A special law assigned the position of 'county' to the city of Zagreb. Local bodies shall carry out affairs of local jurisdiction which directly address the needs of citizens and, in particular, the affairs related to the organization of settlements and housing, physical and urban planning, utility services, child care, social welfare, primary health care, education and basic education, culture, physical culture and sport, technical culture, consumer protection, protection and improvement of the environment, fire protection and civil protection.[29]

27. The regional government is in charge of activities of local (regional) significance; in particular, affairs related to education, health, physical and urban planning, economic development, transport and transport infrastructure and the development of a network of educational, health, social and cultural institutions. Affairs of local and regional jurisdiction shall be regulated by law. At the allotment of these affairs, priority will be given to bodies which are closest to the citizens. In determining the scope of local and regional governments, one should take into account the scope and nature of affairs and the requirements of efficiency and economy (Article 129a of the Constitution).

28. Local and regional governments are entitled, under the law, to independently regulate the internal organization and jurisdiction of their bodies and adapt them to local needs and opportunities, through their statutes.[30] In performing the affairs within their jurisdiction, units of local and territorial self-government are independent and subject only to the control of constitutionality and legality by the authorized State bodies.[31] Local and regional governments have the right to their own revenues which they freely use in the performance of affairs within their jurisdiction. Revenues of local and regional governments must be proportional to their authorities provided by the Constitution and law. The State is obliged to help the financially weaker municipalities in accordance with the law.[32]

6. Judicial System

29. The Croatian judicial system was envisioned by the Courts Act (CA).[33] The courts protect the Constitution, international treaties and legally established order of Croatia and ensure uniform application of the law and the equality of all before the law. Courts rule in respect of the fundamental rights and duties of citizens, the rights and obligations of Croatia and its local and regional governments and the rights and obligations of other legal entities. They impose sanctions and other measures against perpetrators of criminal acts and offences established by law and other regulations, decide on the legality of general and individual acts of public bodies,

29. Article 129a of the Constitution.
30. Article 129b of the Constitution.
31. Article 130 of the Constitution.
32. Article 131 of the Constitution.
33. Courts Act, Official Gazette [OG] No. 28/13, 33/15, 82/15, 82/16.

resolve disputes on personal relations of citizens, labour, commercial, property and other civil disputes and make decisions in other legal matters when so prescribed by law.[34]

30. In Croatia, judicial power is exercised by regular and specialized courts as well as the Croatian Supreme Court. The ordinary courts are municipal courts and district courts. Specialized courts are commercial courts, administrative courts, magistrates' courts, the High Commercial Court of the Republic of Croatia, the High Administrative Court of the Republic of Croatia and the High Misdemeanour Court of the Republic of Croatia. The highest court in the Republic of Croatia is the Croatian Supreme Court.[35] Municipal courts solve non-contentious and enforcement cases, resolve probate cases, handle land register cases and keep the land registry, decide on the recognition and enforcement of foreign judgments, are charged with international legal assistance in procedures in their jurisdiction, carry out international judicial cooperation with the EU Member States in proceedings under its jurisdiction.[36] County courts carry out investigative and notary disciplinary proceedings for disciplinary offences and decide on these offences in the first instance or, when it is stipulated by law, decide on appeals against decisions of the disciplinary proceedings because of irregularities in the performance of notaries cases as stipulated by law. County courts also perform tasks of mutual legal assistance in procedures in their jurisdiction, carry out international judicial cooperation with EU Member States in the procedures within its competence, carry out the execution of foreign criminal decisions and perform other duties specified by law.[37]

31. The commercial courts act in registration matters and lead court water usage registers, decide on enrolment in the register of ships and yachts, decide on the limitation of liability of the shipowner, decide on the proposals in connection with the establishment, operation and termination of a company, decide in non-contentious matters prescribed by the Companies Act, carry out the procedure of recognition of foreign court decisions and arbitral awards in commercial disputes, implement the preservation of evidence for procedures for which they are competent, determine security measures in processes and procedures, decide on the proposals for the opening of bankruptcy proceedings and carry out bankruptcy proceedings, perform duties of international legal assistance in the taking of evidence in commercial matters and perform other duties specified by law.[38] The High Commercial Court decides on appeals against decisions that are made in the first instance by commercial courts, resolves conflicts of territorial jurisdiction between commercial courts, decides on the transfer of jurisdiction between commercial courts and performs other duties specified by law.[39]

34. Article 3 of the CA.
35. Article 14 of the CA.
36. Article 18 of the CA.
37. Article 19 of the CA.
38. Article 21 of the CA.
39. Article 24 of the CA.

32. Administrative courts decide on appeals against individual decisions of public bodies, decide on complaints against the conduct of a public law body, decide on claims for the inaction of public legal bodies within the prescribed deadline, decide on actions taken against administrative contracts or the execution of administrative contracts and other cases prescribed by law.[40] The High Administrative Court of the Republic of Croatia decides on appeals against judgments of the administrative courts and the decision against which an appeal is permitted, determines the legality of general Acts, decides on conflicts of jurisdiction between administrative courts and in other cases prescribed by law.[41]

33. Magistrates' courts issue rulings in the first instance on offences unless misdemeanour law prescribes the subject matter as falling within the jurisdiction of another body. They perform duties of international legal assistance in procedures in their jurisdiction and other duties specified by law.[42] The High Misdemeanour Court decides on appeals against decisions of misdemeanour courts and State administration bodies of the first instance and appeals against the decisions of other authorities when prescribed by a special law, on the conflict of jurisdiction between magistrates' courts, decides on extraordinary legal remedies and performs other duties specified by law.[43]

34. The Croatian Supreme Court, as the highest judicial body in the Republic of Croatia, ensures the uniform application of the law and the principle of equality. It decides on regular legal remedies when prescribed by a special law or on extraordinary legal remedies against final decisions of the courts in the Republic of Croatia. It resolves conflicts of jurisdiction when it is prescribed by a special law, discusses current issues of judicial practice, analyses the need for professional training of judges, court advisors and judicial trainees and performs other duties specified by law.[44]

7. State Attorney

35. The State Attorney's Office is an autonomous and independent judicial body authorized and obliged to act against the perpetrators of criminal and other offences, to undertake legal actions to protect the assets of Croatia and to provide legal remedies in order to protect the Constitution and the law. The State Attorney General of the Republic of Croatia is appointed for a term of four years by *Sabor* at the proposal of the Croatian government, with the prior opinion of the competent committee of *Sabor*. The Deputy Public Prosecutors, in accordance with the Constitution and law, are appointed and relieved by the State Attorney Council.[45] In criminal

40. Article 22 of the CA.
41. Article 25 of the CA.
42. Article 23 of the CA.
43. Article 26 of the CA.
44. Article 20 of the CA.
45. Article 121a of the Constitution.

cases, the competent State Attorney's Office acts against the perpetrators of crimes that are prosecuted ex officio or at the initiative of the State, and to achieve this function it has the powers and duties prescribed by law. The competent State Attorney represents the Republic of Croatia in all proceedings conducted in order to protect its property rights and interests before the courts, administrative and other bodies unless the law or a decision of the competent State authority determines otherwise. This is prescribed by the State Attorney's Act (SAA).[46]

8. Ombudsmen

36. The system of the Ombudsman is extremely important for the legal system of the Republic of Croatia. In addition to the Ombudsman, there are also the Children's Ombudsman, the Ombudsman for Gender Equality and the Ombudsman for Persons with Disabilities. The Ombudsman is appointed by *Sabor* in order to promote and protect the human rights and freedoms enshrined in the Constitution, the laws and the international legal instruments on human rights and freedoms adopted by the Republic of Croatia. Anyone can complain to the Ombudsman if they consider that, as a result of unlawful or improper work of State bodies, local or regional governments or public authorities, his or her constitutional or legal rights are threatened or violated. The Ombudsman is elected by *Sabor* for a term of eight years. The Ombudsman is independent in his or her work. The Ombudsman and other commissioners of *Sabor* for the promotion and protection of human rights and fundamental freedoms have immunity as Members of *Sabor*.[47] The Ombudsman for Children protects, monitors and promotes the rights and interests of children on the basis of the Croatian Constitution, international treaties and laws. The Ombudsman for Children acts independently and autonomously, adhering to the principles of justice and morality. The Ombudsman for Children is appointed and dismissed by *Sabor* at the proposal of the Croatian government.

37. The rights and obligations of the Ombudsman for Children are prescribed by the Ombudsman for Children Act (OCA).[48] The Ombudsman for Children: monitors the compliance of laws and other regulations in the Republic of Croatia relating to the protection of rights and interests of children with the provisions of the Croatian Constitution, the Convention on the Rights of the Child and other international documents relating to the protection of rights and interests of children; monitors the fulfilment of obligations of the Republic of Croatia arising from the Convention on the Rights of the Child and other international documents relating to the protection of rights and interests of children; monitors the application of regulations relating to the protection of rights and interests of children, the violation of

46. State Attorney's Act, Official Gazette [OG] No. 76/09, 153/09, 116/10, 145/10, 57/11, 130/11, 72/13, 148/13, 33/15, 82/15.
47. Article 93 of the Constitution.
48. Ombudsman for Children Act, Official Gazette [OG] No. 73/17.

individual rights of children and studies general occurrences and manners of violation of rights and interests of the child; advocates for the protection and promotion of the rights and interests of children with special needs; proposes measures for a comprehensive system to protect and promote the rights and interests of children and to prevent harmful activities jeopardizing the rights and interests of children; informs the public on the rights of children; and performs other duties specified by law.[49]

38. The Gender Equality Act (GEA)[50] prescribes the rights and obligations of the Ombudsman for Gender Equality. The Ombudsman for Gender Equality is appointed by *Sabor* at the proposal of the Croatian government. The Ombudsman and his/her deputy are Croatian officials, appointed for a term of eight years, and may be reappointed. The Ombudsman and his/her deputy must be of different genders and one of them shall have a graduate degree in Law. The Ombudsman and his/her deputy shall be Croatian citizens who have completed a graduate-level university study and whose personal endeavours are known to the public in the field of human rights.[51] The Ombudsman for Gender Equality: receives complaints from any natural person or legal entity regarding discrimination in the field of gender equality; provides assistance to individuals and legal persons who filed a complaint of sexual discrimination when instituting legal proceedings; investigates individual complaints prior to the submission of the lawsuit; carries out a mediation process with the ability to reach a settlement; collects and analyses statistical data on cases of gender discrimination; conducts independent surveys concerning discrimination; publishes independent reports; and exchanges available information with corresponding European bodies.[52]

39. The rights and obligations of the Ombudsman for Persons with Disabilities are prescribed by the Ombudsman for Persons with Disabilities Act (OPDA).[53] The Ombudsman for Persons with Disabilities shall be appointed and dismissed by *Sabor* at the proposal of the Croatian government. He or she has two deputies who are appointed and dismissed by *Sabor* at the proposal of the Ombudsman for Persons with Disabilities. Both the Ombudsman for Persons with Disabilities and his/her deputy are Croatian officials, appointed for a term of eight years, and may be reappointed.[54] The Ombudsman for Persons with Disabilities: monitors the compliance of laws and other regulations, in the Republic of Croatia, relating to the protection of the rights and interests of persons with disabilities, with the provisions of the Croatian Constitution and international documents relating to the protection of the rights and interests of persons with disabilities; monitors the execution of the obligations of Croatia arising from international documents relating to the protection of the rights and interests of persons with disabilities; monitors the implementation of policies, national strategies and programmes of Croatia related to the

49. Article 7 of the OCA.
50. The Gender Equality Act, Official Gazette [OG] No. 82/08, 69/17.
51. Article 20 of the GEA.
52. Article 19 of the GEA.
53. Ombudsman for Persons with Disabilities Act, Official Gazette [OG] No. 107/2007.
54. Article 4 of the OPDA.

protection of the rights and interests of persons with disabilities; cares for the protection of human rights and fundamental freedoms of people with disabilities, combating all forms of discrimination because of a disability; considers cases of violations of the rights of persons with disabilities; informs the public about violations of the rights of persons with disabilities and takes action to prevent them; advocates for the protection and promotion of the rights and interests of persons with disabilities; proposes taking measures to build a comprehensive system of protection and promotion of the rights and interests of persons with disabilities; proposes measures aimed at improving the quality of life of people with disabilities; proposes measures aimed at improving the quality of life of families of disabled people; collects information and informs the public on the rights of people with disabilities; and performs other duties specified by law.[55]

9. Agencies

40. In parallel with the increasing number of regulatory agencies in Europe, there are now more than seventy-five agencies in Croatia. Defining what constitutes regulatory agency is a very complex task, a task that is suffering from uncertainty and depends on factors such as the type of the study, the country where the research is conducted and the theoretical framework of research.[56] In Croatia, Koprić and Musa recognize two main types of agencies: the regulatory agencies and the executive agencies (a third, less important, kind are called expert agencies[57]). Regulatory agencies are established by law as legal persons with public authority whose task is to regulate a specific sector.[58] Executive agencies cover a wide range of agencies in the economic and non-economic sectors with a variety of tasks, from making individual decisions to license, to financing programmes, to provide various services, etc.[59] The purpose of expert agencies is to support the design and monitoring of the implementation of the policy performance of expert-analytical activities.[60]

41. Staničić claims that there are five conditions that a legal person must meet to be considered a regulatory agency. These conditions are: that there must be a legal entity with public authority outside of the State administration; that it has to have the power to issue general Acts; lead individual administrative procedures; that there must be no appeal against the individual decisions of the regulatory agencies; and that they are established by law and report to the legislature authorities.[61] Accordingly, regulatory agencies that operate in Croatia are: the Croatian Agency

55. Article 6 of the OPDA.
56. Musa, A., Agencies in Croatia: Something Old or Something New?, HKJU – CCPA, 2 (2013): 389.
57. Koprić, I., Musa, A., What Kind of Agencification in Croatia? Trends and Future Directions, Transylvanian Review of Administrative Sciences, Special Issue 2011: 38.
58. *Ibid.*
59. *Ibid.*
60. *Ibid.*
61. Staničić, F., Current Questions of Framework and Action of Regulatory Agencies in the Republic of Croatia (*Aktualna pitanja ustroja i djelovanja regulatornih agencija u Republici Hrvatskoj*), *The Fourth Skopje-Zagreb Colloquium* (*Četvrti skopsko-zagrebački kolokvij*), Skoplje 2013: 65.

for Supervision of Financial Services; the Agency for Electronic Media; the Agency for Railway Safety; the Croatian Regulatory Authority for Network Industries; the Croatian Energy Regulatory; and the Agency for Public Private Partnerships.

10. Croatian National Bank

42. The Croatian National Bank is the Central Bank of the Republic of Croatia. For the realization of its objective and in carrying out their tasks, the Croatian National Bank has legal personality, according to the Croatian National Bank Act (CNBA).[62] The Croatian National Bank is autonomous and independent in the framework laid out by the Constitution and laws in all activities within its jurisdiction, which is particularly reflected in: the formulation and implementation of monetary and foreign exchange policy; the holding and management of the international reserves of Croatia; the issuance of banknotes and coins and issuance and revocation of licenses and approvals in accordance with the laws governing the operations of credit institutions, credit unions, payment institutions, electronic money institutions and payment systems and foreign exchange operations and operations of authorized transmissions; the performance of supervision and control in accordance with the laws governing business of credit institutions, credit unions, payment institutions, electronic money institutions and payment systems; the management of accounts of credit institutions and performing payment transactions on those accounts; the issuing loans to credit institutions and receiving deposits from credit institutions; regulating and improving the payment system; the performance of tasks provided by law for the Republic of Croatia; issuing general Acts on operations within its competence, contributing to the stability of the financial system as a whole; and the performance of other tasks as provided by law.[63]

43. In achieving its objective and carrying out its tasks the Croatian National Bank may, without prejudice to their goal, their autonomy and independence, cooperate with the Croatian government and other State authorities and, within its competence, take measures to promote this cooperation. The Croatian government submits to the Croatian National Bank all proposals and reports relating to the objective, tasks and duties of the Croatian National Bank, including draft decisions and regulations of the Croatian government and legislative proposals prior to their submission to *Sabor*, on which the Croatian National Bank may issue an opinion (Article 6 of the CNBA).

II. Geography and Population

44. The Republic of Croatia is a Central European and Mediterranean country, with an area of 56,594 square kilometres. Within this area, as estimated in mid-2012, live 4.3 million inhabitants, with an average population density of 75.4 people

62. Croatian National Bank Act, Official Gazette [OG] No. 75/08, 54/13.
63. Article 4 of the CNBA.

per square kilometre. This population statistics indicate a continuing decline since 1991 when the census showed a total of 4,784, 265 inhabitants.[64] It has land borders with Slovenia, Hungary, Serbia, BiH and Montenegro, and the maritime border is shared with Italy. Territorial organization of the Republic of Croatia consists of counties, cities and municipalities. The Republic of Croatia consists of 21 counties – 20 counties plus the city of Zagreb, which has the status of a county. Croatia has 127 towns and 429 municipalities.[65] For a country of only 56,594 square kilometres and 4,105,493 inhabitants, the number of local and regional units are very high. Therefore, reform of local and regional government is often mentioned. However, fundamental reform is still pending.

45. The official language of the Republic of Croatia is Croatian, and the official script is the Latin alphabet. In parts of the country with a significant minority population, minority languages are in use (Italian in Istria and Serbian and the Cyrillic script in the east of the country). Croats make up 90.4% of the Croatian population; the most common of the national minorities are Serbs (4.4%). Bosnians make up 0.7% of the population, 0.6% of the population is undeclared, 0.6% is determined according to regional affiliation and 3.3% is unknown.[66] As far as religious representation is concerned, 86.3% of the population profess to be Roman Catholic, 4.4% are Orthodox Christian, 3.8% are atheists, 2.2% did not answer, 1.5% are Muslims, 1% are unknown and 0.8% are agnostics.[67]

III. Social and Cultural Values

46. According to the Constitution, the Republic of Croatia is formed as a sovereign and democratic State in which the freedom and rights of people, as well as their economic and cultural progress and social welfare, are guaranteed.[68] Freedom, equality, national equality and gender equality, peace, social justice, respect for human rights, inviolability of ownership, conservation of nature and the environment and a democratic multiparty system are the highest values of the constitutional order of the Republic of Croatia.[69] In reality, the Republic of Croatia is (still) a transitional society. Although it can be considered that the transition from communism to democracy was formally completed with the accession of the Republic of Croatia to NATO and the EU, some elements of the communist heritage remain. Badly managed privatization of State-owned property has led to a significant drop in industrial production which, in turn, led to great distrust in the capitalist system and unrealistic 'nostalgia' for Yugoslavia in certain parts of the population. There is a significant lack of confidence in the justice system as a result of the dependence of the judiciary on the Communist Party in the previous regime.

64. Croatia in numbers [*Hrvatska u brojkama*], study of the Croatian Statistics Bureau, available at: http://www.dzs.hr/Hrv_Eng/CroInFig/croinfig_2013.pdf (2 Mar. 2015).
65. *Ibid.*
66. *Ibid.*
67. *Ibid.*
68. Preamble to the Constitution.
69. Article 3 of the Constitution.

47. Religion plays a major role in the social life existing in the Republic of Croatia, 92.2% of the citizens declaring themselves as religious (86.3% Catholic, Orthodox 4.4%, 1.5% Muslims). Although the number of practical believers is certainly significantly lower, it cannot be denied that there is a significant influence of religious communities (especially the Catholic Church) on social issues. This is confirmed by the recent successful referendum in which the Constitution was changed to define marriage as a union of man and woman.

§2. The Media Landscape

I. Overview of the Media Markets and Main Actors

A. Introduction

48. The media landscape of the Republic of Croatia has significantly changed since the declaration of independence. The main reasons for the changes are twofold. The first relates to the change in the social system; namely, in the Communist SFRY, all media (printed, TV, radio) were State-owned and significantly censored. Today, the vast majority of media are privately owned. Another reason for the significant changes is technological development; namely, with the development of the Internet and mobile communications, the traditional media that dominated the twentieth century slowly but certainly lost importance. So, print media have, for years, lost circulation and revenue. Television, as a medium, is still relevant but with significantly lower ratings, while the way radio is used and listened to has changed significantly. Technological changes have made the Internet an extremely important information medium and have led to an increase in the importance of websites as a means of information consumption. Below, I will showcase the main media categories in the Republic of Croatia; print media, TV, radio, as well as websites as a new generation of media.

B. Print Media

49. The most important printed media in the Republic of Croatia can be divided into daily and weekly papers. The daily newspapers are *Jutarnji list* from Zagreb, *Novi list* from Rijeka, *Slobodna Dalmacija* from Split, *Večernji list* from Zagreb, *Glas Slavonije* from Osijek, *24 sata* (*24 hours*) from Zagreb, *La Voce del Popolo* from Rijeka, *Sportske novosti* from Zagreb, *Poslovni dnevnik* from Zagreb, *Metro Express* from Zagreb and *Zadarski list* from Zadar. The papers with the largest circulation are *24 hours* (90,000 copies), *Večernji list* (49,500 copies), *Jutarnji list* (50,000 copies), *Slobodna Dalmacija* (35,000 copies), and *Novi list* (20,000 copies).[70]

70. The Croatian Journalists' Association (CJA), Circulation of daily newspapers in constant fall, available at: http://www.hnd.hr/naklade-dnevnih-novina-u-konstantnom-su-padu (22 Dec. 2017).

50. Ownership of print media is completely private. The only printed media owned by the State used to be *Vjesnik*, but it was shut down in 2012. In the print media market of the Republic of Croatia in general, two publishers are owners of the vast majority of print media – *Hanza Media d.o.o.* and *Styria Media Group AG*. *Hanza Media d.o.o.* is a domestic publishing house owned by Marijan Hanžeković, which publishes *Jutarnji list, Slobodna Dalmacija, Sportske novosti* and a whole range of regional newspapers and weekly magazines. *Styria Media Group AG* is one of the largest Austrian media companies based in Graz. It owns several Croatian daily newspapers such as *Večernji list, 24 sata* and *Poslovni dnevnik*. Important weekly papers are *Glas Koncila, Nacional* and *Privredni vjesnik*. *Glas Koncila* is a Catholic weekly published by the Croatian Catholic Church. It is considered an unofficial paper of the Croatian Catholic Church. *Nacional* is a political weekly issued by *NCL Media Group*, with a circulation of about 20,000 copies, and *Globus* is a political weekly published by *Hanza Media*, with a circulation of about 28,000 copies.[71]

C. Television

51. Ten channels with national concession are currently available in Croatia. *HTV1, HTV2, HTV3* and *HTV 4* are public television channels. *Nova TV, Doma TV, RTL, RTL 2, Sport TV* and *Croatian Music Channel* are private channels. There are also 20 channels with local or regional concessions. Alternative distribution platforms (IPTV, satellite) are available for about 600 channels of various profiles.[72] Over the last decade, the ratings of individual channels have changed considerably. *Nova TV*, coming from the last place among the four channels with a national concession in 2010, became the most watched channel in prime time (19–23 hours), retaining its primacy by the end of 2012, and even further increasing its lead.[73] A similar trend is observed in daytime viewership, where *Nova TV* became the most watched in 2011. The biggest decline in ratings compared to 2006 can be found in *HTV1* and *HTV2* followed by *RTL*.[74]

52. Since 2008, the Croatian TV market has recorded a continuous drop in revenue from marketing activities. It has lost more than 22% in value. Internet advertising is the only market that has had continuous growth in the observed period, and the impact of this market on the total advertising market has become significant, It has a grown for more than 800%, from HRK 30 million in 2008 to HRK 245 million in 2017 (*See* Table 1).[75] According to global examinations, the Croatian TV advertising market is prone to seasonal trends where, in the summer months, the number of hours spent in front of the TV is reduced by up to 20% on average and,

---

71. *Ibid.*
72. Electronic Media Agency, TV Market Analysis, available at: http://www.e-mediji.hr/files/repozitorij/Analiza_TV_trzista.pdf (22 Dec. 2017).
73. *Ibid.*
74. *Ibid.*
75. The Croatian Association of Communications Agencies (HURA), www.hura.hr.

accordingly, there is not much revenue from large advertiser sales. The largest TV advertisers in the Republic of Croatia come from the same industry as is the case in the global TV advertising market, namely telecommunications, pharmaceuticals and consumer goods.[76]

Table 1 Value of Advertising Market (in millions HRK) – Data Compiled by The Croatian Association of Communications Agencies (HURA)

Year	*TV*	*Radio*	*Press*	*Out of Home*	*Rest*	*Internet*	*Total*
2008	950	250	785	220	20	30	2,255
2009	790	225	615	165	20	35	1,850
2009 vs 2008	–17%	–10%	–22%	–25%	0%	17%	–18%
2010	770	213	545	151	20	36	1,735
2010 vs 2009	–3%	–5%	–11%	–8%	0%	3%	–6%
2011	765	190	457	140	15	83	1,650
2011 vs 2010	–1%	–11%	–16%	–7%	–25%	131%	–5%
2012	702	163	384	135	12	90	1,484
2012 vs 2011	–8%	–14%	–16%	–4%	–20%	8%	–10%
2013	685	125	300	130	11	107	1,388
2013 vs 2012	-2%	-23%	-14%	-4%	-8%	19%	-7%
2014	715	132	307	126	10,6	117	1,408
2014 vs 2013	4%	6%	-7%	-3%	-4%	9%	1%
2015	740	130	275	128	11	168	1,452
2015 vs 2014	3.5%	–1.5%	–10.4%	1.6%	0%	43.6%	3.1%
2016	758	128	252	130	11	214	1,493
2016 vs 2015	2%	–2%	–8%	2%	0%	27%	2.8%
2017	741	127	218	130	10	245	1,473
2017 vs 2016	–2.2%	–0.4%	–13.3%	0.3%	–7.8%	14.5%	–1.4%

Sources MediaPuls (IpsosPuls), AGB Nielsen, FINA, Medijske agencije HURA-e.

53. The downturn in the TV advertising market has been made somewhat more serious due to the fact that during the digitization process, new terrestrial broadcasting televisions emerged on the national level in 2010, and the even more modest share in the audience has further influenced the fragmentation of the TV advertising market on the national level.[77] Reduced broadcasting costs after switching to digital

76. *Ibid.*
77. *Ibid.*

broadcasts for existing commercial broadcaster TV channels (*Nova TV* and *RTL*) has facilitated the launch of new specialized TV channels for which the listed publishers received concessions in 2010 and launched entertainment channels *Doma TV* and *RTL 2*.[78] Broadcasting of two TV channels further reinforced the influence of commercial publishers by enabling them to access advertisers by selling their reach to audiences through two channels, thereby ensuring a parallel reach to a wide audience through the general channel and targeted audiences through a specialized channel.[79]

54. New Croatian TV channels such as *24sata.tv*, *Narodna TV*, *Arena Sport* and *Mini TV* were gradually added to the TV advertisers market, along with the penetration of channels on other platforms (IPTV and cable) and, thus, further complicated the issue of securing revenue from the sale of advertising space to existing national TV channels.[80] With the introduction of a new pay TV service on the Croatian market through terrestrial broadcasting platforms, triple-play package offerings and a recent decision by HAKOM to deregulate the price of basic pay TV services provided by significant market power operators (*T-HT* and *ISKON*), as well as a recent purchase of *B.net* and *DigiTV* by *Vipnet*, the preconditions were created for additional growth in the telecommunications market.[81]

D. Radio

55. A total of 84.5% of the population listens to the radio, with the vast majority of listeners listening to the radio from 6 am to 6 pm and less than 10% of radio listeners listen in the late evening.[82] More than half of the listeners most frequently listen in the early morning and early afternoon hours. Men (38.5%) more than women (29.8%) listen to the radio in the early morning hours, i.e., from 6:00 am to 10:00 am in the morning.[83] 47.3% of the listeners over the age of 70 usually listen to the radio in the early morning hours, as well as 19.9% of young listeners.[84]

56. On average, listeners listen to the radio for two hours a day. Listeners aged 35 to 44 and listeners between 55 and 70 years listen to the radio for more than two hours per day.[85] People in Dalmatia listen to the radio for about an hour and a half daily, while listeners in Northern Croatia listen to the radio for on average three hours a day.[86] Listeners form Zagreb listen to the radio for about two and a half

---

78. *Ibid.*
79. *Ibid.*
80. *Ibid.*
81. *Ibid.*
82. Radio Market Analysis, Ipsos Connect, available at: https://www.e-mediji.hr/hr/pruzatelji-medijskih-usluga/istrazivanja-i-analize/analiza-radijskog-trzista/ (23 Dec. 2017).
83. *Ibid.*
84. *Ibid.*
85. *Ibid.*
86. *Ibid.*

hours a day.[87] People listen to the radio mostly in the car (31%) or by a stand-alone radio receiver (29.9%).[88] The younger population, up to 24 years, is more likely to use mobile phones (13.1%) and computers and laptops (6.4%) more frequently than other age groups for radio listening.[89]

57. Public radio broadcast stations include *HR-1*, *HR-2*, *HR-3*, *Radio Dubrovnik*, *Radio Knin*, *Radio Osijek*, *Radio Pula*, *Radio Rijeka*, *Radio Sljeme*, *Radio Split* and *Radio Zadar* and a number of smaller local radio stations.[90] According to *MediaPuls* data, for the period from November 2015 to January 2016, the daily reach of the public radio service was 13.5% (meaning that 13.5% of citizens age 10 to 74 listen to these stations at least five minutes a day). The weekly reach of the specified radio stations is 29.2%.[91] There were differences between regions, both in the weekly and in the daily reach of the specified radio stations. The daily reach is less than 10% (and the weekly less than 20%) in the regions of Northern Croatia, Slavonia and Lika and Banovina.[92] A somewhat bigger reach exists in the area of Zagreb and Dalmatia, where this reach has been largely achieved on the basis of *Radio Sljeme* in Zagreb, or *Radio Split* in Dalmatia.[93] The largest reach of public radio service is realized in Istria and the Croatian Littoral, where the weekly reach is over 50%.[94] As in the regions of Zagreb and Dalmatia, this reach is largely carried by one radio station and, in the case of Istria and the Croatian Littoral, the radio station in question is *Radio Rijeka*, whose weekly reach is 38.6%.[95]

58. The most important private radio stations with a national concession are *Narodni Radio* and *Otvoreni Radio*, which have a significantly higher audience than public radio services. Also, from regional private radio stations, it is necessary to distinguish *Radio Antena* in the Zagreb area and *Radio Dalmacija* in the Split-Dalmatia County.

E. Electronic Publications

59. Publications of print or TV media outlets (*Styria, Hanza Media, RTL*) are among the most visited Croatian web pages.[96] In 2017, news portal *Index.hr* was the most visited among other electronic publications with 55% of visits in a week,

87. *Ibid.*
88. *Ibid.*
89. *Ibid.*
90. *Ibid.*
91. *Ibid.*
92. *Ibid.*
93. *Ibid.*
94. *Ibid.*
95. *Ibid.*
96. Electronic publication market analysis, available at: https://www.e-mediji.hr/hr/pruzatelji-medijskih-usluga/istrazivanja-i-analize/objavljena-analiza-trzista-elektronickih-publikacija/ (23 Dec. 2017).

and the only independent company that isn't owned by an established media company.[97] The second most visited electronic publication is *24sata.hr* with 54% of visits in a week. Furthermore, *jutarnji.hr* with 46%, *dnevnik.hr* with 39% and *net.hr* with 38% readers visits in a week.[98] Taking into account all twenty published publications, users who visit an electronic publication on their personal computer tend to return eight times on average. The frequency of returning to a website and the time spent on them is a sign of loyalty to a particular publication.[99]

60. The market is dominated by companies whose electronic publishing is a subsidiary activity, i.e., their core activity is related to other media.[100] Thus, 52.5% of revenue from electronic publications is owned by print publishers and 9.6% by companies that produce and broadcast television programmes.[101] The share of Internet service providers is also significant (10.5%), while companies specializing in online production captured 27.3% of revenue from electronic publications.[102] At the same time, revenue from electronic publications is only a marginal source of revenue, according to the share of total revenue, for companies whose core business is providing Internet services, television and radio.[103] For print publishers, this share is above 5%, i.e., it is significant, and will likely grow, in line with the growth in the use of electronic publications.[104] On the other hand, revenues from electronic publications account for half of the total revenue of companies who are not active in other media activities or provide Internet access services.[105]

II. Broadcasting Infrastructure

A. *Introduction*

61. Broadcasting infrastructure in the Republic of Croatia has undergone significant changes in the last ten years. TV and radio signals were broadcast exclusively by terrestrial signals. The analogue signal has been steadily replaced by DVB-T, as well as the Internet, as a signal transmission medium. Also, the development and expansion of mobile communications technologies enabled the development of mobile Internet infrastructure. Below we will show all the abovementioned technology for signal transmission in the Republic of Croatia, and their importance for the media in the Republic of Croatia.

97. *Ibid.*
98. *Reuters Institute for the study of Journalism Digital News Report 2017, http://po.st/lfJFXh* (23 Dec. 2017).
99. *Ibid.*
100. *Ibid.*
101. *Ibid.*
102. *Ibid.*
103. *Ibid.*
104. *Ibid.*
105. *Ibid.*

B. DVB-T

62. After switching off analogue transmitters, there are today two basic technologies for distributing TV content: DVB (Digital Video Broadcast) and IPTV.[106] DVB technology is a one-way transmission of compressed image and sound content from the transmitter to the receiver.[107] Depending on the selection of the compression matrix, it may be any standard, but the most commonly used is MPEG-2[11] or MPEG-4[12]. DVB has three basic subversions that depend on the transmission mode from the transmitter point to the receiver: DVB-T (terrestrial), DVB-C (cable) and DVB-S (satellite).[108]

63. DVB technology requires the transmission of the entire multiplexed content (e.g., ten or more TV channels) from the transmitter point to the receiver, which selects the viewing channel.[109] IPTV technology allows sending only one selected TV channel from the transmitter point to the receiver, which also provides significant savings in the required transmission capacity over DVB technology.[110] DVB technology has been developed as a continuation of classical analogue transmission technology in the digital world. The basic task was to utilize the digitalization capabilities to make the frequency bandwidth more efficient while at the same time raising the quality of the received picture and sound signal.[111] DVB has provided the possibility of replacing the previous analogue transmission technology with a digital bandwidth, with the use of an analogue bandwidth for the transmission of an entire multiplex which, depending on compression and quality, can transmit four or more digital TV channels.[112]

64. In Croatia, it was decided that the terrestrial digital network transmitters would use MPEG-2 compression because of the speed of digital broadcasting.[113] Such a decision made it difficult to introduce HDTV and increase the broadcasting price for publishers. It will be necessary to think about switching to MPEG-4.[114] DVB technology does not provide the possibility of feedback and data flow from the user to the operator/publisher but therefore ensures a much higher quality and safer reception of TV signals than IPTV technology.[115]

106. Electronic Media Agency, TV Market Analysis, available at: http://www.e-mediji.hr/files/repozitorij/Analiza_TV_trzista.pdf (23 Dec. 2017).
107. *Ibid.*
108. *Ibid.*
109. *Ibid.*
110. *Ibid.*
111. *Ibid.*
112. *Ibid.*
113. *Ibid.*
114. *Ibid.*
115. *Ibid.*

C. Internet Access

65. Internet access services are provided by a large number of ISPs: Akton, Amis Telekom, ANTENA J.D., ABSOLUTE, AT&T HRVATSKA, ALFA TELEKOM, B.Net Hrvatska, BT Net, CANDOR, CONSILIUM, Cogent Internet, ELVIN, Fenice Telekom, FRISD, GAZO, GLOBAL NET GRUPA, H1 Telekom, Hrvatski Telekom, Hrvatska elektroprivreda, IBM Hrvatska, Iskon Internet, KRK SISTEMI, MAGIC TELEKOM, Metronet telekomunikacije, Nexcom, Novi net, NET PROJEKT, Odašiljači i veze, OPTIKA KABEL TV, OT – Optima Telekom, ORBIS TELEKOM, Primatel, PONDI, Selec, Softnet, S.B., TELE2, TEHNICORE, VIPnet, Voljatel telekomunikacije, VOX, WIMAX Telecom. The operators with the largest market share are Hrvatski Telekom, Vipnet, Metronet telekomunikacije and TELE2. Broadband Internet access is available in the following ways: xDSL access via copper pair; access via mobile networks (EDGE, UMTS, HSDPA); fixed wireless access (Homebox, WiMAX, Wi-Fi Hot-Spots) cable networks; access via leased lines (different from xDSL access via copper pairs, fixed wireless access and access via fibre-optic cables); fibre-optic access (FttH); and satellite access.[116]

66. ADSL access via copper pair enables high-speed downstream and lower-speed upstream and is suitable for high-speed data transfer and access to related content, with the transmission rate depending on length and type of pair. ADSL retail-level technology is appropriate for Internet search and the use of multimedia services that require greater bandwidth per user.[117] In the Republic of Croatia, the largest number of copper pairs is owned by *Hrvatski Telekom*, which is a former monopoly and owner of the public electronic communications network with the largest number of active copper pairs.[118] The geographic availability/broadness of these copper pairs is very broad because *Hrvatski Telekom* as a universal service provider is obliged to offer all users access to their network.[119] *Hrvatski Telekom*'s access network was built over a long period of time while *Hrvatski Telekom* was a public company and in the further period in which it enjoyed exclusive rights.[120] Broadband Internet access via ADSL is offered by other operators also but by wholesale access to HT's network. The number of users providing broadband Internet access via ADSL technology with direct access to their own network is negligible.[121]

116. HAKOM Broadband Market Analysis, available at: https://www.hakom.hr/UserDocsImages/2012/odluke_rjesenja/IZ-AT-AN-OPR-Analiza%20tržišta%20maloprodaje%20širokopojasnog%20pristupa%20Internetu-v1.0.pdf (23 Dec. 2017).
117. *Ibid.*
118. *Ibid.*
119. *Ibid.*
120. *Ibid.*
121. *Ibid.*

D. *Mobile*

67. In the Republic of Croatia, mobile communications services are provided by three operators: *Hrvatski Telekom, Vipnet* and *TELE2*. The mobile communications market in 2016 was exceptionally saturated, with 4,414,347 mobile connections, which is larger than the estimated population of the Republic of Croatia. *Hrvatski Telekom* has the largest market share (47.62%).[122] *Vipnet* has a market share of 34.72%, while *TELE2* is at 17.66%. 51.83% of users use prepaid services, while prepaid subscriptions account for 48.17% of users.[123] Total revenues from services in the mobile communications network in the third quarter of 2017 amounted to HRK 1,153,658,009, which means that the market at the annual level is about HRK 4.5 billion.[124]

III. Technological and Economic Developments on the Media Markets

A. *Introduction*

68. Technological and media development in the media market has been significant in the last ten years. Technological development is primarily related to the new standards and methods of transmission of signals in digital media, while economic development has primarily involved a constant drop in the circulation of printed media and the growing proliferation and importance of electronic media. Nevertheless, the most significant development is noticed in media convergence.

B. *Convergence*

69. People use social media in an ever-increasing capacity.[125] According to data published by Google, in March 2013, 90% of smartphone users use sequentially multiple devices for access to social media, of which seventeen minutes on average on mobile phones, forty-three minutes on tablets, thirty-nine minutes on laptops and forty-three minutes on desktop computers.[126] From year to year, there are noticeable shifts in how we use multimedia content. 56% of users of smart mobile devices use them to watch videos, and 82% use them as their primary news source.[127] In such media convergence, the biggest loser is the printed medium, followed by television.

---

122. Available at: https://www.hakom.hr/default.aspx?id=60 (27 Dec. 2017).
123. *Ibid.*
124. HAKOM Report for Q3 2017, available at: https://www.hakom.hr/UserDocsImages/2017/e_trziste/Tromjesečni%20usporedni%20podatci%20za%20tržište%20elektroničkih%20komunikacija%20RH,Q32017.pdf (27 Dec. 2017).
125. TV Market Analysis, available at: http://www.e-mediji.hr/files/repozitorij/Analiza_TV_trzista.pdf (27 Dec. 2017).
126. *Ibid.*
127. *Ibid.*

70. As a result of this shift in consumer habits, the content is also changing. For example, there are quite a few new formats of professional videos for mobile devices and computers that cover content from news to movies and short documentaries.[128] The trend of watching television and surfing the Internet is also noticeable, according to the latest indicators, as many as 85% of smartphone or tablet owners surf the Internet and watch TV simultaneously once a month, while 40% do it every day.[129] Currently, about 1.5 million smartphones are in use in Croatia, with a significant growth rate that is expected to reach a maximum of 80% of users in the next three years.[130] Apart from the fact that the mobile phone (smartphone) and tablet are becoming the central place for news, weather and social communications including photography, video and music, smartphones and tablets are transformed into TV consumption devices by IPTV.[131] *Max TV To Go* and *B.net Za Van* are examples of such services. This trend will continue at an even faster pace of development in the upcoming period.[132] Traditional media will be facing even greater and higher quality multimedia competition on the Internet.[133]

71. According to data provided by HAKOM penetration of broadband Internet in Croatia in March 2013 was 29.81%, which is significantly less than the most developed countries such as Norway (83%) and South Korea (97%).[134] The average penetration in Western countries is passing 70% penetration.[135] This rapid Internet development has created technical and commercial prerequisites for the emergence of new forms of media services in which content owners can achieve direct access to the end user globally via the Internet.[136] In doing so, the technical quality and viewing experience sometimes outgrow the traditional distribution platforms of radio and television, while the added value for the user is interactivity, mobility and the ability to access the content on any device connected to the Internet at any time.[137] This phenomenon represents another thorough change that the electronic media industry faces. Aggregators such as Google, Netflix, YouTube, as well as terminal equipment manufacturers such as Samsung, LG and others started buying media rights, and in such a transformation it is quite possible that consumers will soon be able to watch some exclusive content only if they own a specific manufacturer's Internet-connected TV.[138] Netflix currently has about 36 million subscribers around the world offering movies, series, documentaries and other content in HDTV standard in non-linear form and linear TV channels via OTT technology on devices

---

128. *Ibid.*
129. *Ibid.*
130. *Ibid.*
131. *Ibid.*
132. *Ibid.*
133. *Ibid.*
134. *Ibid.*
135. *Ibid.*
136. *Ibid.*
137. *Ibid.*
138. *Ibid.*

such as: Smart TV, PC, Mac, IPTV Set Top Box, Tablet PC, smartphone, PlayStation console, Wii console, etc.[139] It remains to be seen how traditional TV publishers will be in the new so-called connected environment.[140]

§3. Sources of Media Law

72. The most important legal sources of substantive media law in the Republic of Croatia are the Media Act (MA),[141] the Electronic Media Act (EMA)[142] and the Electronic Communications Act (ECA).[143] MA governs the prerequisites for the exercise of the principle of freedom of media, journalists' rights on the freedom of reporting and access to public information, the rights and obligations of publishers, the transparency of ownership, the right to correction and reply, market competition and the rights and obligations of other legal and natural persons acting in the field of public information. EMA regulates the rights, obligations and responsibilities of legal and natural persons performing the activities of providing audio and audiovisual media services and electronic publishing services (electronic publications) via electronic communication networks and the interest of the Republic of Croatia in the field of electronic media, while the ECA regulates the area of electronic communication, the use of electronic communications networks and the provision of electronic communications services, the provision of universal services and the protection of the rights of users of services, the construction, installation, maintenance and use of electronic communications infrastructure and associated equipment, market conditions and the rights and obligations of participants in the market of electronic communication networks and services, addressing, management of the radio frequency spectrum, digital radio and television, data security and electronic communications security, inspection and professional supervision and control in electronic communications, as well as the establishment of a national regulatory body for electronic communications and postal services, its organization, scope and jurisdiction, and decision-making and settlement of disputes in electronic communications. Therefore, each of these laws regulates a specific field of media activity as well as the infrastructure for providing the services in question.

73. Basic procedural provisions for legal regulation of the provision of media services, also for the legal protection of users, are contained in the basic procedural provisions of Croatian administrative law, the Administrative Procedure Act (APA)[144] as well as the Administrative Disputes Act (ADA).[145] APA regulates the basic administrative procedure of the Republic of Croatia, which in media law will

139. *Ibid.*
140. *Ibid.*
141. Media Act, Official Gazette [OG] No. 59/04, 84/11, 81/13.
142. Electronic Media Act, Official Gazette [OG] No. 153/09, 84/11, 94/13, 136/13.
143. Electronic Communications Act, Official Gazette [OG] No. 73/08, 90/11, 133/12, 80/13, 71/14, 72/17.
144. Administrative Procedure Act, Official Gazette [OG] No. 47/09.
145. Administrative Disputes Act, Official Gazette [OG] No. 20/10, 143/12, 152/14, 94/16, 29/17.

be especially important when awarding concessions. ADA regulates judicial protection against administrative acts of competent State bodies such as the Electronic Media Agency. Judicial protection is therefore ensured before the administrative courts of the Republic of Croatia. In addition to the above-mentioned basic laws, Croatian law recognizes the entire spectrum of sectoral laws regulating specific areas of media law, the list of which is listed below.

I. Constitution

74.

Constitution of the Republic of Croatia (*Ustav Republike Hrvatske*, Official Gazette [OG] No. 56/90, 135/97, 8/98, 113/00, 124/00, 28/01, 41/01, 55/01, 76/10, 85/10, 05/14).

II. Laws

75.

Electronic Media Act (*Zakon o elektroničkim medijima*, Official Gazette [OG] No. 53/09, 84/11, 94/13, 136/13).
Media Act (*Zakon o medijima*, Official Gazette [OG] No. 59/04, 84/11, 81/13).
Croatian Radio-Television Act (*Zakon o Hrvatskoj radioteleviziji*, Official Gazette [OG] No. 137/10, 76/12, 78/16, 46/17, 73/17).
Electronic Communications Act (*Zakon o elektroničkim komunikacijama*, Official Gazette [OG] No. 73/08, 90/11, 133/12, 80/13, 71/14, 72/17).
Concessions Act (*Zakon o koncesijama*, Official Gazette [OG] No. 69/17).
Audio-visual Activities Act (*Zakon o audiovizualnim djelatnostima*, Official Gazette [OG] No. 76/07, 90/11).
Unauthorised Advertising Act (*Zakon o nedopuštenom oglašavanju*, Official Gazette [OG] No. 43/09).
Act on Restricting the Use of Tobacco and Related Products (*Zakon o ograničavanju uporabe duhanskih i srodnih proizvoda*, Official Gazette [OG] No. 44/17).
Games of Chance Act (*Zakon o igrama na sreću*, Official Gazette [OG] No. 7/09, 35/13, 158/13, 41/14, 143/14).
Copyright and Related Rights Act (*Zakon o autorskom pravu i srodnim pravima*, Official Gazette [OG] No. 167/03, 79/07, 80/11, 125/11, 141/13, 127/14, 62/17).
Administrative Procedure Act (*Zakon o općem upravnom postupku*, Official Gazette [OG] No. 47/09).
Administrative Disputes Act (*Zakon o upravnim sporovima*, Official Gazette [OG] No. 20/10, 143/12, 152/14, 94/16, 29/17).

III. Regulations

76.

Regulation on criteria and increasing the volume of European audiovisual works by independent producers (*Pravilnik o kriterijima i načinu povećanja opsega udjela europskih audiovizualnih djela neovisnih proizvođača*, Official Gazette [OG] No. 77/15).

Regulation on criteria and the increasing of the scope of European works (*Pravilnik o kriterijima i načinu povećanja opsega udjela europskih djela*, Official Gazette [OG] No. 77/15).

Rules on the Grant of Unused Exclusive Rights (*Pravila o ustupanju neiskorištenih isključivih prava*, Official Gazette [OG] No. 47/15).

Regulation on protecting minors in electronic media (*Pravilnik o zaštiti maloljetnika u elektroničkim medijima*, Official Gazette [OG] No. 28/15).

Regulation on detailed criteria for the determination of audiovisual and/or radio programmes considered as own production (*Pravilnik o detaljnim mjerilima za određivanje audiovizualnih i/ili radijskih programa koji se smatraju vlastitom proizvodnjom*, Official Gazette [OG] No. 132/14).

Regulation on Minimum Terms for Performing Audio and Audiovisual Media Services and Keeping Record (*Pravilnik o minimalnim uvjetima za obavljanje audio i audiovizualnih medijskih usluga i vođenju očevidnika*, Official Gazette [OG] No. 83/14).

Regulation on the Register of Providers of Media Services, Electronic Publications and Non-Profit Producers of Audiovisual and/or Radio Programme (*Pravilnik o upisniku pružatelja medijskih usluga, elektroničkih publikacija i neprofitnih proizvođača audiovizualnog i/ili radijskog programa*, Official Gazette [OG] No. 34/13, 79/14).

Regulation on the Fund to Encourage Pluralism and Variety in Electronic Media (*Pravilnik o Fondu za poticanje pluralizma i raznovrsnosti elektroničkih medija*, Official Gazette [OG] No. 150/13, 2/17).

Regulation on Content and Procedure of Notification of Intent to Grant a Concession for Performing the Activities of Providing Media Television and Radio Services (*Pravilnik o sadržaju i postupku obavijesti o namjeri davanja koncesija za obavljanje djelatnosti pružanja medijskih usluga televizije i radija*, Official Gazette [OG] No. 131/13).

Regulation on the amount and manner of payment of fees (*Pravilnik o visini i načinu plaćanja naknada*, Official Gazette [OG] No. 93/13).

Rules for Right to Correction in Audio and Audiovisual Media Services Providers (*Pravila za ostvarivanje prava na ispravak u programima pružatelja audio i audiovizualnih medijskih usluga*, Official Gazette [OG] No. 46/10).

Regulation on Croatian Audio-visual Works (*Pravilnik o hrvatskim audiovizualnim djelima*, Official Gazette [OG] No. 43/10).

IV. Relevant International Acts

77. Directive 2010/13/EU of the European Parliament and of the Council of 10 March 2010 on the coordination of certain provisions laid down by law, regulation or administrative action in the Member States concerning the provision of audiovisual media services (Audiovisual Media Services Directive (AVMSD)) (Text with European Economic Area (EEA) relevance).

Part I. Freedom of Speech

Chapter 1. Constitutional Framework

78. There are several legal concepts in the Croatian Constitution which are relevant in the context of opinions and expressions of opinions. In essence, one should differentiate between freedom of thought, freedom of opinion and freedoms of speech, expression and the media. All of these freedoms are recognized by the Constitution; however, they do not enjoy the same level of protection. For the purposes of this monograph, it is necessary to differentiate between freedom of thought (*'sloboda misli'*) and freedom of opinion (*'sloboda mišljenja'*),[146] on one side, and freedom of expression, speech, media and information, on the other. The first of these rights are part of the *forum internum* of every individual and should enjoy absolute protection. On the other side, we find freedoms of expression, speech, media and information, as well as the prohibition of censorship. These rights are relative, meaning that they can be restricted, in accordance with the Constitution. Their scope and possible restrictions are discussed below.

79. In addition to constitutional rules, in the context of the Croatian media law a special role is given to the European Convention for Human Rights (ECHR), for two reasons. Firstly, Croatian law follows a monist system in relation to international treaties.[147] According to the Article 141 of the Constitution, 'international treaties which have been concluded and ratified in accordance with the Constitution, published and which have entered into force shall be a component of the

---

146. It should be noted that the Constitution recognizes and protects both the freedom of thought and the freedom of opinion. Although there is no case law on this matter, it is argued in legal literature that the term *freedom of thought* protects one's *ability to think freely*, by prohibiting any intervention or experiment on mentally healthy persons which would interfere with his or her cognitive processes. On the other hand, *freedom of opinion* covers the freedom to *hold opinion without interference*, which means that the State is prohibited from forcing individual to change his opinion (negative duty), and also has obligation to protect individual from similar interferences by other private parties (positive duty).

See Alaburić, V., *Sloboda misli, mišljenja, izražavanja i informiranja*, [Freedom of Thought, Expression and Information], *Hrvatska pravna revija* [Croatian Law Review] 3 (6) (2003): 1–7.

According to the Article 17(3) of the Constitution, freedom of thought is one of the absolute values of legal order, and consequently cannot be restricted, not even in cases of clear and present danger to the existence of the state. Freedom of opinion, on the other hand, is not explicitly recognized as absolute right in the Constitution. Although there is no case law on this matter, it is argued in the legal literature that the freedom of opinion enjoys that same (absolute) status as the freedom of thought (Alaburić, p. 5).

147. Smerdel, B., Sokol, S., *Ustavno pravo* [Constitutional Law] (2009): 101.

domestic legal order of the Republic of Croatia and shall have primacy over domestic law. Their provisions may be altered or repealed only under the conditions and in the manner specified therein or in accordance with the general rules of international law'. Since Croatia is party to the ECHR (since 1997), provisions of this convention, as interpreted by the ECtHR, are directly applicable in Croatian legal system. This connection between Croatian law and the ECHR is additionally emphasized by the MA, which explicitly stipulates in its Article 1(2) that its provisions must be applied and interpreted in line with the ECHR.

80. Both the Constitution and the MA, on the normative level, create a strong obligation for national courts to pay due attention to the principles developed in the case law of the ECtHR. However, it is questionable whether and to what extent this obligation is fulfilled in practice. On the one side, in its more recent judgements, the Croatian Constitutional court is increasingly quoting various ECtHR case law. Although the Constitutional Court could be criticized for selectively following ECtHR's case law and while it has at the same time been criticized in domestic legal scholarship for failing to develop its own systematic approach in freedom of expression cases,[148] this should still generally be viewed as a positive development. On the other side, Croatian courts of the first and second instance are much more reluctant to rely directly on the ECtHR's case law. For example, it seems that ordinary courts sometimes struggle with recognizing the importance of certain speech for a public debate in a democratic society and follow the overly formalistic approach in the interpretation of legal texts.

81. Finally, when analysing the scope and limitations of freedom of expression, one must also take into account the constitutional provisions regarding (1) restrictions of fundamental rights and freedoms,[149] (2) some other fundamental rights such as the rights to private and family life, dignity, reputation,[150] privacy of communications,[151] as well as protection of personal data,[152] and (3) the prohibitions of incitement to war, violence or hatred. These provisions will be discussed below.

148. Ljubić, D., *Ustavna zaštita prava na slobodu misli i izražavanja mišljenja* [Constitutional Protection of the Right to Freedom of Thought and Expression], *Hrvatska pravna revija* [Croatian Law Review], 14 (11) (2014): 9.
149. Articles 16 and 17 of the Constitution.
150. Article 35 of the Constitution.
151. Article 36 of the Constitution.
152. Article 37 of the Constitution.

Chapter 2. Article 38 of the Constitution

§1. Scope of the Freedom of Expression and Freedom of Speech

82. In the Republic of Croatia, freedom of speech is a part of the broader right to freedom of expression. Article 38 of the Constitution expressly recognizes both the freedom of expression and freedom of speech. Article 38(1) of the Constitution guarantees freedom of thought and expression; Article 38(2) further stipulates that freedom of expression encompasses particularly freedom of the press and other media, freedom of speech and public opinion and free establishment of all institutions of public communication.

83. Freedom of expression is guaranteed for all natural and legal persons. With regards to freedom of expression of legal persons, there is no case law of the Constitutional court, but since Croatia is party to the European Convention on Human Rights all of the relevant case law of the European Court of Human Rights applies. Furthermore, Article 76 of the Constitution provides deputies in the Croatian Parliament with legal immunity for actions done or statements made in the course of their legislative duties. The article further stipulates that no deputy shall be held criminally liable, detained or sentenced for an opinion expressed or a vote cast in the Croatian Parliament. A deputy may be detained without approval from the Croatian Parliament only if he has been caught in the perpetration of a criminal offence carrying a sentence of imprisonment exceeding five years. In such a case, the Speaker of the Croatian Parliament shall be notified thereof. According to Article 34 of the Act on the Government of the Republic of Croatia[153] the same regime is applied to all members of the Croatian government (prime minister and ministers), which stipulates that criminal proceedings for criminal offence carrying a sentence of imprisonment not exceeding five years cannot be conducted against members of the government during the course of their mandate, without prior approval of the Croatian government.[154]

§2. Freedom of the Press and Other Media

84. Freedom of the media is explicitly recognized as one of the aspects of the freedom to expression due to the role of the media in a democratic society.[155] The scope of this freedom is defined in Article 3 paragraph 2 of the MA as covering, in particular, 'freedom of the expression of opinion, independence of the media; freedom to collect, research, publish and disseminate information for the purpose of public informing; pluralism and diversity of media, free flow of information and

153. Act on the Government of the Republic of Croatia, Official Gazette [OG] No. 150/11, 119/14, 93/16.
154. Article 34 of the Constitution.
155. Rajko, A., *Domašaj ustavne odredbe o zabrani cenzure* [Reach of the Constitutional Norm on the Prohibition of Censorship], *Hrvatska pravna revija* [Croatian Law Review], 8 (12) (2008): 1.

openness of the media to different opinions, beliefs and various contents, accessibility of public information; respect for the protection of human personality, privacy and dignity; freedom to establish legal persons for the performance of activities in public informing, printing and distribution of press and other media from the country and abroad, production and publishing of radio and television programme, as well as other electronic media; autonomy of editors, journalists and other authors of programme contents in accordance with the professional codex'.

85. The aforementioned principles are reinforced by Article 4 paragraph 1 of the MA, which stipulates that no one is allowed to influence programme content of the media by coercion or through the abuse of power, nor to restrict freedom of media in any other manner. Furthermore, Article 3 of the EMA stipulates that freedom of expression and full programme freedom of electronic media must be guaranteed where no provision of EMA may be construed in such a manner that it provides the right to censorship or limitation of the freedom of speech and expression of thought.[156]

§3. Prohibition of Censorship

86. The Croatian Constitution stipulates in its Article 38(3) that 'censorship shall be forbidden', without defining the term 'censorship'. In addition, the precise meaning of this provision was never analysed by the Constitutional Court. In such circumstances, it is suggested in legal literature that prohibition of censorship for purposes of Article 38(3) should encompass 'any power of the public authority to decide whether and to what extent materials containing information or ideas can be imported, distributed or published, as well as the factual execution of such control without formal authorization to do so'.[157]

87. Another issue which remains unresolved is the status of the prohibition of censorship, namely whether it is of absolute or relative character. According to opinions expressed in legal literature, censorship is not a form of ordinary restriction of a fundamental right, which could be imposed in accordance with the usual three-step test of Article 16 (basis in law – legitimate aim – proportionality). Instead, it is argued that the only way to impose such measure is on the basis of Article 17, which is applicable only during a state of war, or when there is a clear and present danger to the independence and unity of the State, or in case of natural disasters.[158]

88. Moreover, leading scholars of constitutional law have emphasized the dangers of self-censorship due to defamation law and brought this in relation to the constitutional prohibition of censorship.[159] However, in its two decisions from 1996 and 2000, the Constitutional Court explicitly refused to take into account the possibility

156. Article 3 of the EMA.
157. Rajko, *Domašaj ustavne odredbe o zabrani cenzure*, *supra* note 155, p. 4.
158. *Ibid.*, p. 6.
159. Smerdel, Sokol, *supra* note 147, p. 138.

that certain criminal law legislation might lead to self-censorship. Firstly, in 1996 the Constitutional Court refused to accept the argument that ex officio criminal prosecution for offences of insult or defamation against persons in the highest public offices might encourage self-censorship, with the explanation that such a provision is not censorship, and that 'the term self-censorship is not even used' in the Constitution.[160] Four years later, the Constitutional Court reversed itself and declared the same provision unconstitutional, essentially on the basis that there are no valid reasons for different treatment of highest officials and ordinary citizens when it comes to prosecution of insult and defamation. However, while doing so, the Court once again refused to accept arguments based on the likelihood of self-censorship and chilling effects. According to the Court, 'due to the subjective nature of self-censorship, understood as controlling expressions of one's thoughts and emotions in a manner and to the extent determined by their author, it is not possible to determine, in a legally valid and objective manner, whether certain provision of law leads to self-censorship or chilling effects on freedom of expression. From the constitutional perspective, assumptions about such effects are not sufficient to declare a provision of law unconstitutional'.[161]

§4. Right of Access to Information

I. General Introduction

89. In 2010, the Constitution of the Republic of Croatia was amended in order to include the right of access to information (Article 38(4) of the Constitution). According to this provision, the right of access to information held by any public authority shall be guaranteed. Furthermore, it is prescribed that any restriction of this right must be (1) stipulated by law, (2) proportionate to the nature of the need for such restriction in each individual case and (3) necessary in a free and democratic society.

90. On the legislative level, access to information by media enjoys dual legal protection. On the one hand, the MA contains, since 2004, several provisions enabling journalists to access public information. On the other hand, several months before the MA was promulgated, the Croatian Parliament passed a general freedom of information Act – Access to Information Act from 2003 (Croatian: *Zakon o pravu na pristup informacijama*).[162] In 2013, the Parliament passed a completely new Access to Information Act (AIA 2013), which is currently in force.[163] Both the MA and the AIA 2013 ensure the right to access public information. In addition, AIA 2013 also enables reuse of such information.

---

160. Decision of the Constitutional Court No. U-I-274/1996 of 10 July 1996. *See also* Rajko, *Domašaj ustavne odredbe o zabrani censure*, *supra* note 155, p. 7.
161. Decision of the Constitutional Court No. U-I-241/2000 of 10 May 2000. *See also* Rajko, *Domašaj ustavne odredbe o zabrani censure*, *supra* note 155, p. 7.
162. Access to Information Act 2003, Official Gazette [OG] No. 172/2003, 144/2010, 37/2011, 77/2011.
163. Access to Information Act 2013, Official Gazette [OG] No. 25/2013, 85/2015.

II. The Notion of Public Information

91. Under the AIA 2013, public information is defined as any data held by a public authority in any form and on any medium. For the purposes of this Act, public authorities are organs of the State and State administration bodies, units of local and regional self-government and persons vested with public authorities.

92. On the other hand, the MA defines public information as 'any information held by bodies of executive, legislative or judicial power, bodies of local and regional self-government units, as well as by other legal and natural persons performing public service or duty, and *which pertains to their work and activities*'. In other words, the subject matter of the right of access to information is defined more broadly under the AIA 2013 than under the MA.

III. Principles of the Right to Access to Information

93. The AIA 2013 follows a free access principle. Under Article 6, the beneficiary of the right of access to information is every natural and legal person, whether Croatian or foreign. Furthermore, according to Article 18(4) of the AIA 2013, the person who submits a request for access to information is not obliged to state reasons for that request, nor is he required to make reference to the provisions of the AIA 2013.

94. Under Article 7 of the AIA 2013, public authorities are required to provide information in a timely manner. Furthermore, the provided information must be complete and accurate. Identical requirements are stipulated in Article 6(1) of the MA.

95. Article 8 of the AIA 2013 introduces the principle of equality in access to information. Under this provision, public authorities are required to provide information to all beneficiaries in an equal manner and under the same terms. Specifically, public authorities are not allowed to put some beneficiaries in an unequal position, especially by enabling them to obtain information before others or in a manner that provides them with favourable treatment. Similar to the equality principle of the AIA 2013, the MA prescribes in its Article 6(2) that public information should be accessible to all journalists under the same terms.

Chapter 3. Restrictions of the Right to Freedom of Speech

96. Freedom of expression is not an absolute right. According to Article 10(2) of the ECHR, this right carries with it certain responsibilities. As such it may be subject to *formalities*, *conditions*, *restrictions* or *penalties* which are (1) prescribed by law, (2) pursue a legitimate aim[164] and are (3) necessary in a democratic society. In the Croatian legal system, freedom of expression can be restricted in accordance with the rules stipulated in Article 16 of the Constitution, which follows an approach similar to the three-step test, as used in Article 10(2) of the ECHR. In essence, the Constitution requires that any restriction of the right to freedom of expression (1) has a legal basis in the law, (2) pursues legitimate aims (protection of legal order, public morals, health and rights and freedoms of others) and (3) is proportionate to the aims pursued, in each individual case.

97. The desire to bring Croatian law in line with the ECHR is also evident from Article 3(3) of the MA. This article contains provisions which correspond completely to the ECHR's Article 10(2) and stipulates that 'limitations to the freedom of the media shall be permitted only when and to the extent necessary in a democratic society in the interest of national security, territorial integrity or public peace and order, prevention of disorder or criminal acts, protection of health and morality, protection of the reputation or rights of others, prevention of disclosing confidential information or for the purpose of preserving the authority and impartiality of the judiciary, solely in a manner stipulated by law'.

§1. Prohibition of Hate Speech

98. One general restriction on the freedom of media is stipulated in Article 3(4) of the MA, according to which 'it shall be prohibited to transmit programme contents in the media which incite or glorify ethnic, racial, religious, gender or other inequality or inequality on the basis of sexual orientation, as well as ideological and state creations on the basis of such foundations, and to provoke ethnic, racial, religious, gender or other animosity or intolerance, animosity or intolerance on the basis of sexual orientation, to incite violence and war'. Similarly, Article 12 of the EMA stipulates that in audio or audiovisual media services it is prohibited to promote, or favour the promotion of the spreading of hatred or discrimination based on race or ethnic affiliation or colour, gender, language, religion, political or other belief, national or social origin, property, trade union membership, education, social status, marital or family status, age, health condition, disability, genetic heritage,

164. According to Art. 10(2) of the ECHR, freedom of expression can be restricted in the interests of national security, territorial integrity or public safety, for the prevention of disorder or crime, for the protection of health or morals, for the protection of the reputation or rights of others, for preventing the disclosure of information received in confidence, or in order to maintain the authority and impartiality of the judiciary.

native identity, expression or sexual orientation, as well as anti-Semitism, xenophobia and the ideas of totalitarian regimes such as fascism, nationalism and communism.[165]

§2. Protection of Rights and Freedoms of Others

99. Moreover, Article 35 of the Constitution of the Republic of Croatia stipulates that everyone should enjoy respect for, and legal protection, of their private and family life, dignity and reputation. Similarly, the MA in its Article 7(1) recognizes that every person has the right to the protection of privacy, dignity, reputation and honour. The term *privacy*, which is not used in the Constitution, is defined in the MA (Article 2) as meaning 'personal and family life, and above all, the right to life according to one's own choice and option'. Therefore, the meaning of *privacy* in the MA is within the scope of *private and family life*, as protected by the Constitution.

100. According to Article 7(1) of the MA, everyone enjoys the right to privacy. At the same time, MA imposes certain restrictions to this right. Firstly, it is stipulated that a person performing a public service or duty has the right to the protection of privacy, *except in cases related to the public service or duty that he or she performs* (MA Article 7(2)). Secondly, 'a person who draws public attention by his/her statements, behaviour and other acts relating to his/her personal or family life may not request the same level of the protection of privacy as other citizens' (MA Article 7(3)). Finally, Article 8 of the MA stipulates that 'there shall be no violation of the right to the protection of privacy if in relation to the published information a justified interest of the public prevails over the protection of privacy with regard to the journalist profession or information'.

§3. Right to Correction

101. According to Article 38(5) of the Constitution, every person whose legally recognized rights have been violated by public communication shall have the right to correction. Right to correction and right to replay are also further regulated within MA and EMA and are covered in respective chapters of this monograph.

165. Article 12 EMA.

Part II. Regulation of Print Media

Chapter 1. Journalists' Profession

§1. Notion

102. Croatian law does not differentiate between journalists on the basis of media outlets with which they are associated, for example, print and other media. Consequently, a journalist is everyone who collects, processes, designs or classifies information for *media*, which, according to Article 2, paragraph 2 of the MA, includes 'newspapers and other print media, radio and television programmes, programmes of newspaper agencies, electronic publications, teletext and other forms of daily or periodical publishing of editorial programme contents through the transmission of recording, voice, tone or picture'.

103. Although the term itself was widely used in national legislation, the notion of 'journalist' was not legally defined until the new Media Acts of 2003 and 2004 were enacted. According to Article 2, paragraph 8 of the MA, a journalist is a natural person who is involved in collecting, processing, designing or classifying information for publishing through the media and is employed with the media publisher on the basis of an employment contract, or performs journalist activities as an independent profession, in accordance with law. Essentially, two categories of journalists are recognized in Croatian law. Firstly, there are journalists who are associated with a particular media publisher by virtue of an employment contract. Secondly, there are journalists who perform their activities as independent professionals, that is to say, outside of an employment relationship (freelancers).

104. Although there are several schools of journalism in Croatia, a person does not need to hold any particular degree in order to work as a journalist.

§2. Journalists' Associations

I. Croatian Journalists' Association

105. The Croatian Journalists' Association (CJA) was founded on 18 November 1910. It is a member of the International Journalist Federation (IFJ) and the European Journalist Federation (EFJ), and it has more than 2,500 members. The main goals of the CJA are to implement professional interests, ethics and freedom of speech; to promote the public's right to be informed about all current affairs and the right of every person to freedom of speech, opinion and access to public media guaranteed by the Constitution of the Republic of Croatia; to protect the reputation and dignity of journalists; to further protect journalists from publishers' autocracy and prevent monopolization; and, finally, to protect the financial and social status of journalists.

106. To become a member of CJA, journalists must submit their application to the CJA Commission for membership. The application must contain documents that can confirm the professional status of the journalists, with evidence of published articles and a regular income from journalistic activities.

107. Journalists that are members of the CJA must adhere to its Code of Honour.[166] As a basic principle, the Code of Honour stipulates that the right to complete and timely information and freedom of expression are basic rights of every human being, regardless of his or her race, sex, nationality language, religion political or other beliefs, national or social background, birth, education, social status or other characteristics. From that right of the public to know facts and opinions originate all the duties and rights of the journalist. In their practice, journalists are required to defend human rights, dignity and freedom, to respect pluralism of ideas and attitudes, to contribute to strengthening the rule of law and, as a democratic part of the general public, to participate in the control of the activity of appointed and elected officials. A journalist must abide by the Constitution and the positive legislation of the Republic of Croatia, care for culture and the ethics of public expression and respect the achievements and values of a prosperous civilization.

108. Furthermore, the Code of Honour of the CJA deals with the rights and duties of journalists, the flow of information, the protection of basic human rights and freedoms, the free judgement of journalists (where a journalist should not be part of undertakings that can influence their independence, objectivity and free judgement thus impairing journalistic dignity) and editorial responsibilities.

109. The main body that is in charge of implementing the CJA's Code of Honour is the Ethical Council. The organizational structure, composition, the election of members to the Ethical Council and the duties of the Ethical Council are all governed by the Ordinance on work of Ethical Council.[167] All members of the CJA must abide by decisions of Ethical Council, the Code of Honour and said Ordinance.

110. The Ethical Council of the CJA can initiate proceedings against particular journalists and their work, or another person who is acting as a journalist but is *not a member* of the CJA. In the latter case, the Ethical Council will not take a decision

166. Code of Honour of the Croatian Journalists, available at: http://www.hnd.hr/kodeks-casti-hrvatskih-novinara (12 Apr. 2017).
167. Ordinance on work of Ethical Council of the CJA, available at: http://www.hnd.hr/pravilnik-o-radu-novinarskog-vijeca-casti-lipanj (12 Apr. 2017).

of infringement of Code of Honour and respective sanctions, but it will issue an opinion in which it will ascertain which of the ethical and professional principles were infringed.

111. Anybody can initiate a proceeding in front of Ethical Council by submitting a written and signed application. The application must contain a clear explanation of infringement together with evidence, information and circumstances that support the claims of infringement of the Code of Honour and other rules.

112. In the case where the Ethical Council is discussing an infringement on the Code of Honour by a journalist who is a member of the CJA, and after having conducted a discussion and a vote of the members of Ethical Council, it can issue the following sanctions:

- in more lenient cases of the infringement – the Ethical Council issues a *notice* to the journalist that will remind him/her about the obligations and duties to abide by ethical and professional standards;
- in more severe cases of the infringement – the Ethical Council issues a *warning* to the journalist that will warn him/her of this grave infringement of ethical and professional standards;
- in the most severe cases of infringement on the Code of Honour, where the dignity of the profession is endangered – the Ethical Council can take a decision of *exclusion* from CJA.

113. As a legal support structure for its members, the CJA also established a Centre for the protection of freedom of expression (CPFE). The CPFE provides members of the CJA with legal protection. This includes: legal representation (defence) in all civil and criminal proceeding initiated against members because of their published works; legal counselling and representation of journalists in proceedings against publishers; and education and other legal activities that are related to journalists' activities and profession.

II. Trade Union of the Croatian Journalists

114. The Trade Union of Croatian Journalists (TUCJ) was founded on 19 May 1990 with a goal to protect basic labour, social and professional rights of journalists in Croatia. All the journalists and other workers in media companies are eligible to become TUCJ members. This also includes freelancers and retired journalists. TUCJ covers lawyer fees for its members in labour court cases. TUCJ has its subsidiaries in sixty-three media companies in Croatia. In media companies where TUCJ doesn't have its subsidiary, it has individual members. In total, TUCJ has about 3,000 members.

115. TUCJ successfully signed collective agreements with eight major media companies and two local media companies. TUCJ also started collective negotiations with associations of media employers over a Draft Collective Agreement for

Journalists and Media Staff in Croatia but an agreement was not reached. The intention was that with such an agreement at the national level, better protection for journalists and media staff in smaller local media, as well as basic rights for permanent freelance collaborators in the media would be accomplished.

Chapter 2. Journalists' Rights

§1. Role of Journalists as Watchdogs of Society

116. The role of journalists as watchdogs of society in Croatia is especially emphasized in the MA.[168] Freedom of the media shall comprise in particular: freedom of the expression of opinion; independence of the media; freedom to collect, research, publish and disseminate information for the purpose of informing the public; pluralism and diversity of media; free flow of information and openness of the media to different opinions, beliefs and various contents; accessibility to public information; respect for the protection of human personality, privacy and dignity; freedom to establish legal persons for the performance of activities in public informing, printing and distribution of press and other media from the country and abroad, production and publishing of radio and television programme, as well as other electronic media; autonomy of editors in chief, journalists and other authors of programme contents in compliance with the professional codex.[169] Limitations to the freedom of the media shall be permitted only when and to the extent necessary in a democratic society in the interest of national security, territorial integrity or public peace and order, prevention of disorder or criminal acts, protection of health and morality, protection of the reputation or rights of others, prevention of disclosing confidential information or for the purpose of preserving the authority and impartiality of the judiciary solely in a manner stipulated by law.[170]

§2. Journalists' Independence

117. Article 26 of the MA states the following on journalists' independence: 'The relationships between the publisher, the editor-in-chief and the journalists, as well as their mutual rights and obligations, shall be determined by the media statute.[171] The media statute means a self-regulatory act which shall especially determine the manner of journalists' participation in the procedure of appointment and dismissal of the editor-in-chief, the freedom of work and journalists' responsibility, as well as the conditions and procedure pursuant to which the editor-in-chief, editors and journalists have the right to a resignation, along with a fair severance pay, in cases of such changes in the ownership or management structure of the media which lead to significant alterations in the programme basis or programme content of that media (the so-called conscience clause).[172] The statute of the media shall be adopted by the publisher and a journalists' representative, with the prior consent from the majority of the total number of journalists from the media. Journalists shall elect their representative by a majority vote.[173] If the publisher and the journalists'

168. . Media Act, Official Gazette [OG] No. 59/04, 84/11, 81/13.
169. . Article 3 of the MA.
170. *Ibid.*
171. Article 26 of the MA.
172. *Ibid.*
173. *Ibid.*

representative fail to adopt the statute within six months from the beginning of operation of the media, the statute shall be passed, upon the request of the journalists' representative, within three months from the day of receipt of the request, by an arbitration composed of an equal number of representatives of the associations of publishers and of the journalists' associations.[174] The publisher shall be obliged to conclude an agreement with every person s/he orders a journalist contribution from prior to ordering, in compliance with the regulations and media statute. The contract shall also regulate copyrights related to the journalist contribution.[175] A journalists' contribution referred above shall be a published written, verbal, image or online: report, information, comment (notice or comment, social chronicle, article, review), criticism, cartoon, essay, interview, reportage (travelogue, sketch, feature), as well as titles and announcements. A journalist contribution shall also be specialist works and genres, such as editing, photography, photo-news, photo-reportage, photo-editing and photo-cartoon.'[176]

118. A journalist shall have the right to express his standpoint with regard to all events, occurrences, persons, subjects and activities.[177] A journalist's work contract may not be terminated, his salary decreased or his position on the editorial board altered, the contracted income or part thereof decreased or suspended, because of an expressed standpoint.[178] If in case of a dispute a journalist expresses facts which justify the doubt that the termination of the work contract, decrease of salary or altered position on the editorial board or decrease or suspension of the contracted income is the consequence of expressing a standpoint from paragraph 1 of this Article, the burden of proof falls on the publisher.[179]

119. A journalist shall have the right to refuse to prepare, write or participate in the drafting of a report, the content of which is contrary to the rules of the journalists' profession and ethics, about which he will inform the editor-in-chief in writing.[180] If a journalist refuses to act upon order because, by doing so, he would violate the rules of the journalists' profession, the employer may not terminate his work contract, decrease his salary or alter his position on the editorial board.[181] If, in case of a dispute, the journalist expresses facts which justify the doubt that the termination of the work contract, decrease of salary or altered position on the editorial board is the consequence of refusing to act upon orders from paragraph 1 of this Article, the burden of proof falls on the publisher.[182]

174. *Ibid.*
175. *Ibid.*
176. *Ibid.*
177. Article 27 of the MA.
178. *Ibid.*
179. *Ibid.*
180. Article 28 of the MA.
181. *Ibid.*
182. *Ibid.*

§3. PROTECTION OF JOURNALISTIC SOURCES

120. A journalist shall not be obliged to provide data about the source of published information or the information he intends to publish.[183] The right of a journalist referred to in paragraph 1 of this Article shall also pertain to the editor-in-chief, and the editors and authors of published reports who are not journalists.[184] Prior to publication, the journalist shall be obliged to inform the editor-in-chief of the fact that the information is from an unidentified source in the manner stipulated in the media statute. In that case, all the provisions on the protection of the source of information shall also apply to the editor-in-chief.[185] The State Attorney's Office, when such limitations are required in the interest of national security, territorial integrity and protection of health, may lodge a request with the competent court to order the journalist to disclose data on the source of the published information or information he intends to publish.[186]

121. The court may order the journalist to disclose data on the source of the published information or information he intends to publish, if so required for the protection of public interest and if it concerns particularly important and serious circumstances and the following has been indisputably established:

- that a reasonable alternative measure for disclosing data on the source of information does not exist or that the person or body seeking the disclosure of the source of information has already used that measure;
- that legal public interest for disclosing data on the source of information clearly prevails over the interest of protecting the source of information.[187]

When assessing the circumstances of the case, the court shall exclude the public in the course of the procedure of disclosing information and warn the persons present that they are obliged to keep confidential everything they have found out in the procedure as well as of the consequences of disclosing confidential information.[188]

183. Article 30 of the MA.
184. *Ibid.*
185. *Ibid.*
186. *Ibid.*
187. *Ibid.*
188. *Ibid.*

Chapter 3. Journalists' Liability

§1. Liability

122. The publisher who, by publishing information in the media, causes damage to another person shall be obliged to pay compensation, except in cases stipulated below. The publisher shall not be liable for damage if the information which caused the damage is:

- an accurate report from a discussion during the session of bodies of legislative, executive or judicial power and bodies of local and regional self-government units, or at a public gathering, or if it was transmitted from a legal act of bodies of legislative, executive or judicial power or bodies of local and regional self-government units, without changing its meaning by editorial processing;
- published within an authorized interview;
- based on truthful facts or facts for which the author had justified reason to believe that they were truthful and he undertook all necessary measures to verify their truthfulness, while there was a justified interest on the part of the public for the publishing of that information, and if the activity was undertaken in good faith;
- a photograph of the affected party taken in public or a photograph of the affected party taken with his knowledge and consent for publishing purposes, whereby the affected party failed to prohibit the publication, i.e., to restrict the right of the author of the photograph to use the work;
- truthful and the circumstances of the case indicate that the journalist was able to determine in good faith that the affected party agreed with the publication thereof;
- based on the author's value judgements the publication of which was in the public interest and provided in good faith.[189]

123. The above-mentioned shall not pertain to personal data the confidentiality of which is stipulated by law, to information on minors and information collected in an illegal manner. The existence of liability shall be proven by the plaintiff, while the existence of preconditions for the release from liability for damage shall be proven by the defendant.[190] If the information has been authorized, and certain parts thereof contain evident insults or libels, the authorization shall not exclude the joint liability of both the publisher and the editor-in-chief, if they failed to act in good faith.[191]

189. Article 21 of the MA.
190. *Ibid.*
191. *Ibid.*

§2. DEFAMATION AND LIBEL

124. Provisions on defamation and libel can be found in the Civil Obligations Act (COA)[192] and the Criminal Code (CC).[193] Every natural and legal person has the right to protection of his/her personal rights under the presumptions established by law.[194] The right to life, the physical and mental health, reputation, honour, dignity, name, the privacy of personal and family life, freedom and others, are understood under the rights of personality within the meaning of the COA.[195] A legal person has all of the above-mentioned personality rights, other than those relating to the biological essence of a natural person and, in particular, the right to reputation, honour, name, business secret, freedom of business.[196]

125. Whoever insults another shall be punished by a fine of up to ninety daily units.[197] The amount of the daily unit is determined by taking into account the perpetrator's income and assets and the average costs necessary to sustain the perpetrator and his family. The daily amount may not be less than HRK 20 or more than HRK 10,000. Whoever insults another through the press, radio, television, computer system or network, at a public gathering or in some other way, thus making the insult accessible to a large number of persons, shall be punished by a fine of up to one hundred and eighty daily units.[198] If the insulted person returns the insult, the court may remit the punishment of both perpetrators.[199] If the perpetrator was prompted by the improper behaviour of the injured party, or the injured party has accepted his or her apology for the committed offence before the court, the court may remit his or her punishment.[200]

126. Whoever asserts or disseminates, in front of a third party, a factual claim about another person which can damage his/her honour or reputation (defamation), shall be punished by a fine of up to one hundred and eighty daily units.[201] Whoever commits this offence through the press, radio, television, computer system or network, at a public gathering or in some other way, thus making the insult accessible to a large number of persons, shall be punished by a fine of up to three hundred and sixty daily units.[202] There shall be no defamation if the perpetrator proves that the factual claims made or propagated by him/her are true or that there existed a serious reason as to why he or she, acting in good faith, believed them to be true.[203] If the perpetrator did not assert or disseminate the factual claim in the public interest or

192. Civil Obligations Act, Official Gazette [OG] No. 35/05, 41/08, 125/11, 78/15.
193. Criminal Code, Official Gazette [OG] No. 125/11, 144/12, 56/15, 61/15, 101/17.
194. Article 19 of the COA.
195. *Ibid.*
196. *Ibid.*
197. Article 147 of the CC.
198. *Ibid.*
199. *Ibid.*
200. *Ibid.*
201. Article 148 of the CC.
202. *Ibid.*
203. *Ibid.*

for some other justified reason but acted, for the most part, with the aim of dishonouring or damaging the reputation of another person, especially if the claims concern another person's personal or family life, he or she shall not be allowed to prove the above-mentioned circumstances.[204] If the perpetrator admits that his or her claims are not true and retracts them, the court may remit his/her punishment.[205]

127. Whoever knowing that it is untrue, in front of a third party asserts or disseminates a false factual claim about another person which can damage his honour or reputation (intentional defamation), shall be punished by a fine of up to three hundred and sixty daily units.[206] Whoever commits intentional defamation through the press, radio, television, computer system or network, at a public gathering or in some other way, thus making the insult accessible to a large number of persons, shall be punished by a fine of up to five hundred daily units.[207] Criminal offences against honour and reputation shall be prosecuted by private action.[208] If the criminal offences against honour and reputation were committed against a deceased person, criminal proceedings may be instituted by a private action brought by the deceased person's spouse or cohabitant, life partner or informal life partner, parent, child, adopter, adoptee or siblings.[209] The judgment convicting the perpetrator of a criminal offence against honour and reputation which was committed through the press, radio, television, computer system or network, or other media shall be publicly announced in full or in part at the request of the injured party and at the perpetrator's expense.[210] The public announcement shall be made in the manner indicated by the court in the judgment. Whenever possible, the court shall order that the judgment be publicly announced in the same media in which the criminal offence was committed.[211]

§3. PRIVACY

128. The Constitution of the Republic of Croatia guarantees the right to privacy. The freedom and privacy of correspondence and all other forms of communication shall be guaranteed and inviolable.[212] Restrictions necessitated by the protection of national security and the conduct of criminal prosecution may be prescribed solely by law.[213] The safety and secrecy of personal data shall be guaranteed for everyone.[214] Without consent from the person concerned, personal data may be collected,

204. *Ibid.*
205. *Ibid.*
206. Article 149 of the CC.
207. *Ibid.*
208. Article 150 of the CC.
209. *Ibid.*
210. Article 151 of the CC.
211. *Ibid.*
212. Article 36 of the Constitution.
213. *Ibid.*
214. Article 37 of the Constitution.

processed, and used only under the conditions specified by law.[215] Protection of data and oversight of the operations of information systems in the State shall be regulated by law.[216] The use of personal data contrary to the express purpose of their collection shall be prohibited.[217]

129. The most important privacy Act is the Personal Information Protection Act (PIPA).[218] The PIPA regulates the protection of personal data of individuals and the supervision of the collection, processing and use of personal data in the Republic of Croatia.[219] The purpose of personal data protection is the protection of private life and other human rights and fundamental freedoms in the collection, processing and use of personal data.[220] The protection of personal data in the Republic of Croatia is guaranteed to every natural person irrespective of nationality and residence and regardless of race, colour, sex, language, religion, political or other belief, national or social origin, property, birth, education, social status or other features.[221]

215. *Ibid.*
216. *Ibid.*
217. *Ibid.*
218. Personal Information Protection, Official Gazette [OG] No. 103/03, 118/06, 41/08, 130/11, 106/12.
219. Article 1 of the PIPA.
220. *Ibid.*
221. *Ibid.*

Chapter 4. Right to Reply

130. The right to reply is regulated by the MA. The concerned natural or legal person shall have the right to request from the editor-in-chief to publish, free of charge, his response to published information mentioning his name or relating to him directly in some other manner.[222] The response shall refer to a text or message of identical nature as the published information.[223] By way of allegations appropriate for a demonstration of evidence, the response shall, in essence, deny or significantly supplement the allegations of facts and data contained in the published information.[224] The response shall be published without alterations or supplements, with the exception of spelling errors.[225] Before publication, the editor-in-chief shall have the right to request from the author that he or she shortens the response.[226] The editor-in-chief may refuse to publish responses which are equal in terms of content after he has already published the same response.[227] The editor-in-chief may also refuse to publish a response if the response contains false data, claims or allegations inadequate for a demonstration of evidence.[228] If only some data or claims are false or inappropriate for a demonstration of evidence according to the opinion of the editor-in-chief, the editor-in-chief may not refuse publication without previously asking the author to exclude those data and claims from the response.[229]

---

222. Article 56 of the MA.
223. *Ibid.*
224. *Ibid.*
225. Article 57 of the MA.
226. *Ibid.*
227. *Ibid.*
228. *Ibid.*
229. *Ibid.*

Chapter 5. Access to Public Information

§1. Public Documents and Meetings

131. The most important Act regarding access to public information is the Access to Information Act (AIA).[230] Public authority bodies are obliged to publish the following information in an easily searchable and machine-readable format on their websites:

- laws and other regulations relevant to their scope of activity;
- general Acts and decisions they enact, which influence the interests of beneficiaries, together with the reasons for their enactment;
- draft proposals of laws and other regulations and general Acts subject to the public consultation procedures, in accordance with Article 11 of this Act;
- annual plans, programmes, strategies, instructions, work reports, financial reports and other relevant documents referring to activities of the public authority bodies;
- registers and databases or information on registers and databases within their jurisdiction and the manner of access thereto;
- information on public services provided by the public authority, in a visible place, with links to those provided electronically;
- information on financing sources, budget, financial plan or other appropriate documents that determine the revenues and expenditures of public authority bodies, and data and reports on budget execution, financial plans and other appropriate documents;
- information on allocated grants, sponsorships, donations or other aid, including a list of beneficiaries and amounts;
- information on public procurement procedures, tender documents, information on fulfilling the contract obligations, and other information required pursuant to the law governing public procurement;
- information on announced tenders, documents necessary for participation in the tender procedure, and information on the outcome of tender procedures;
- information on the internal organization of public authorities, with the names of persons heading the authority and heads of organizational units with their contact information;
- conclusions from official sessions of public authority bodies and the official documents enacted at these sessions, including information on the work of the formal work bodies within their jurisdiction where decisions are made on the rights and interests of beneficiaries;
- information on the manner and conditions of exercising rights of access to and reuse of information in a visible place, including contact details of the information officer, the necessary forms or links to forms, and the level of fees for access to information and reuse of information;

230. Access to Information Act, Official Gazette [OG] No. 25/13, 85/15.

- responses to frequently asked questions, on the manner of submitting requests by citizens and the media, and other information (news, press releases, data on activities), for the purpose of informing the public about their work and exercising their rights and executing obligations.[231]

132. Public authority bodies are obligated to inform the public of:[232]

- agendas of meetings and sessions of official bodies and their scheduled times, the manner of work and possibilities of direct insight into their work;
- the number of persons who may simultaneously receive direct insight into the work of the public authority bodies, taking account of the sequence of registration.[233]

§2. Court Hearings and Documents

133. The publicity of court hearings differs depending on which type of court proceedings are being conducted. It is, therefore, necessary to present the provisions on civil proceedings, criminal proceedings, misdemeanour proceedings and administrative disputes.

134. The civil procedure is governed by the Civil Procedure Act (CPA).[234] The main hearing is public, but only adults can attend.[235] The court may exclude the public from the entire main hearing or one of its parts if this is required on moral grounds, public order or State security, or for the purpose of safeguarding military, official or business secrets or for the protection of the private life of the parties, but only to the extent that the court considers it unconditionally needed in special circumstances where the presence of the public could be detrimental to the interests of justice.[236] The court can exclude the public where the measures provided for by the CPA would not ensure an undisturbed discussion.[237]

135. The criminal procedure is regulated by the Criminal Procedure Code (CPC).[238] The discussion is public and can be attended by adults.[239] Persons attending the hearing, other than judicial police, may not carry weapons or dangerous tools.[240] The Trial Chamber will exclude the public for the entire hearing or part

231. Article 10 of the AIA.
232. Public authority bodies are not obliged to provide direct insight into their activities in matters from which the public should be excluded.
233. Article 12 of the AIA.
234. Civil Procedure Act Official Gazette [OG] No. 53/91, 91/92, 58/93, 112/99, 88/01, 117/03, 88/05, 02/07, 84/08, 123/08, 57/11, 148/11, 25/13, 89/14.
235. Article 306 of the CPA.
236. Article 307 of the CPA.
237. *Ibid.*
238. Criminal Procedure Code, Official Gazette [OG] No. 152/08, 76/09, 80/11, 91/12, 143/12, 56/13, 145/13, 152/14, 70/17.
239. Article 387 of the CPC.
240. *Ibid.*

thereof: to protect a person under the age of eighteen, at the request of the victim, during his examination as a witness.[241] From the opening of the session to the conclusion of the hearing, the Chamber may at any time, ex officio or at the suggestion of the parties, but always after their examination, exclude the public for the entire hearing or part thereof, if necessary to: protect the security and defence of the Republic of Croatia; protect a secret which would undermine public debate; protect public order and peace; protect the personal or family life of the accused, the victim, the injured party or another participant in the proceedings.[242] Exclusion of the public does not apply to parties, victims, defendants and their representatives.[243]

136. Misdemeanour proceedings are regulated by the Misdemeanour Act (MDA).[244] The law stipulates that public hearings are always public unless the special public provision of the CC excludes the public. Thus, the public will always be excluded in misdemeanour proceedings against a juvenile, and the court may allow the presence of persons involved in protection and upbringing of minors and scientists.[245]

137. The administrative dispute is governed by the ADA. The hearing is public. If this is required in order to protect privacy, the confidentiality of data or other legally prescribed reasons, the court shall exclude the public for the whole hearing or part of it, and the court shall rule on the exclusion of the public by a decision.[246]

---

241. Article 388 of the CPC.
242. *Ibid.*
243. Article 389 of the CPC.
244. Misdemeanour Act, Official Gazette [OG] No. 107/07, 39/13, 157/13, 110/15, 70/17.
245. Article 223 of the MDA.
246. Article 38 of the ADA.

Chapter 6. Press Council

138. The Croatian Media Council was founded in 2011. It was founded by the CJA and the publishers of leading print and electronic media for monitoring and sanctioning violations of journalistic ethics. The Council continued to operate until 2014. Unfortunately, shortly thereafter, the Council was dissolved.

Part III. Regulation of Audio and Audiovisual Media (Broadcasting)

Chapter 1. Public Service Broadcasting

§1. The Concept and Mission of Public Service Broadcasting

139. The Republic of Croatia has a long history in the broadcasting of radio and television. It was one of the first countries in Central and Eastern Europe to establish a radio station, on 15 May 1926. Thirty years later, in 1956, Television Zagreb (the predecessor to Croatian television) started broadcasting its programme. The first live TV broadcast, of the gala opening of the Zagreb Fair, was aired on 7 September 1956, while the first test programmes of Television Zagreb were broadcast on 29 November 1956. After that, constant development of new services and the introduction of new TV and radio channels (in 1972 TV Channel 2; in 1988 TV Channel 3) established Croatian Radio-Television as the most important media outlet in the country. In June 1990, the Croatian Parliament adopted an Act to rename Radio-Television Zagreb to Croatian Radio-Television (*Hrvatska radiotelevizija*: HRT).[247] During the 1990s, HRT had an important role and made a great contribution to coverage of Croatia's War of Independence. Since January 1993, Croatian Radio-Television has been an active member of the European Broadcasting Union (EBU) – the largest organization of Public Service Broadcasters in the world.

140. A transition from analogue to digital broadcasting (DVB-T) began experimentally in May 2002. In 2008, after the government adopted an Analogue to Digital Television Broadcasting Switchover Strategy for the Republic of Croatia,[248] the full digital switchover started, completing the process on 5 October 2010. Today, there are nine main regions of digital TV allotments and additionally some small allotment areas for local digital television stations.

141. Today, public service broadcasting in Croatia is delivered by the Croatian Radio-Television (HRT). HRT was founded by the Republic of Croatia as a legal

247. Croatian Radio-Television Act, Official Gazette [OG] No. 28/1990.
248. Analogue to Digital Television Broadcasting Switchover Strategy for the Republic of Croatia, July 2008, available at: https://www.hakom.hr/UserDocsImages/dokumenti/Analogue%20to%20digital%20television%20broadcasting%20switchover%20strategy%20for%20the%20republic%20of%20Croatia.pdf (14 Feb. 2016).

person, which has a *status of a public institution*. The legal status, operation, organization and financing of HRT are primarily regulated by the Croatian Radio-Television Act (CRTA)[249] and the Statute of HRT, while the broadcasting of its programmes are regulated by the MA, the EMA and its Ordinances, except in the cases where CRTA applies. According to Article 1, paragraph 4 of the CRTA, in its activity, HRT must be independent of any political influence or promoters of commercial interests.

142. Croatian Radio-Television was established to provide public broadcasting services. It performs, produces and broadcasts radio, television, musical and other media-programme content intended to inform, educate, entertain and connect the general national and international public, in accordance with the CRTA.

143. The mission of HRT, as a part of the European cultural heritage of public media services, is to provide services to society, generate public assets and ensure the development of democratic society. With high quality, authoritative and diverse programmes and services, HRT must keep and promote European values and fundamental human rights, and Croatian national and cultural values. HRT must contribute to the development of modern Croatian society and enable each individual to find his/her place in today's surroundings.[250]

The mission objectives of HRT are to:

- create values for society and individuals;
- safeguard, foster and promote national identity and culture;
- promote civil society and the foundations of democracy;
- express diversity and promote tolerance;
- promote knowledge and provide assistance in education, learning and the acquisition of new skills;
- participate in cultural enrichment and in liberating potential;
- promote linkage between the Republic of Croatia and Croatians abroad;
- stimulate creativity and innovation;
- encourage entrepreneurship and have a positive impact on economic trends;
- encourage solidarity and humanity;
- promote media culture and literacy, and to participate in their advancement;
- help people understand the world around them and adapt to changes in modern society;
- represent Croatia, its regions and citizens;
- acquaint Croatia with the world, and the world with Croatia;
- preserve and strengthen the public's trust towards public media services.[251]

249. Croatian Radio-Television Act, Official Gazette [OG] No. 137/10, 76/12, 78/16.
250. The Contract between Croatian Radio-Television and Government of Republic of Croatia for the period 2013–2017.
251. HRT's Business and Development Strategy 2013–2017, available at: http://www.hrt.hr/uploads/media/HRT_s_Business_and_Development_Strategy_2013-2017.pdf (14 May 2017).

144. Furthermore, the concept, mission and main principles of public service broadcasting in Croatian Radio-Television are best noted in three sections of the CRTA. Those three sections are: Programme Principles (Articles 5–8), Definition of Content and Function of Public Service (Articles 9–12); and Transparency and Independence of Work (Articles 16 and 17) of HRT Activities.

I. Programme Principles of HRT

145. In its programmes, HRT must fulfil public interests on State, regional and local level. Its programmes must have an adequate share of informative, artistic, cultural, educational, entertaining, sports and children content.[252] According to Article 6 of the CRTA in its creation of programmes, HRT must promote national interests, contribute to the promotion of human rights, respect privacy, reputation and dignity of each individual, especially children and young people, seniors and disabled people.

146. The main principles in the creation of HRT programmes are:

- equal services for all citizens of the Republic of Croatia;
- credibility and impartiality;
- promotion of national and general values;
- innovation and creativity;
- professionalism and openness;
- technological neutrality;
- media equality;
- responsibility for publicly funded activities;
- promotion of and responsibility for market competition.

II. Definition of Content and Function of Public Service

147. The main task of HRT is to produce and broadcast programmes that inform the public on political, economic, social, health, cultural (such as sports), educational, scientific, religious and ecological topics.

148. In the production and co-production of programmes, according to Article 9 paragraph 5 of the CRTA, HRT has an obligation to foster national audio and audiovisual multimedia creations that contribute to the development of Croatian culture, arts and entertainment, as well as the international representation of Croatian cultural identity.

149. Furthermore, HRT is obligated to support the development of independent production of the audio and video content, ensure high standards in the audio and audiovisual creation of content and promote media literacy programmes.

252. Article 5 of the CRTA.

150. The majority of programmes shown during the course of one year on HRT must be European works. 40% of those programmes must be broadcasted originally in the Croatian language on each general channel of HRT.[253] Also, HRT must allocate at least 15% of its annual budget to procuring European works of independent producers and half of those funds must be intended for works originally produced in the Croatian language.[254]

151. Article 12 of the CRTA stipulates that the share of 'Croatian music' in all of the musical programmes broadcasted by HRT must be at least 40%. Under the CRTA, 'Croatian music' is music that is created by Croatian authors and/or Croatian performers.

III. Transparency and Independence of Work

152. According to Article 16 of the CRTA, HRT must take care of and promote public interests, and be 'responsible to the public' in its activity. Responsibility to the public, as well as the influence of the public on HRT's activity, is exercised especially:

- by the appointment procedure of the Programme Council of HRT, its public work and its task to represent and protect the interests of the listeners and viewers;
- through HRT's obligation to timely and truthfully inform the public on the performance of its activity, as well as its duty to inform the users of its services in a suitable manner on the conditions and manner of service provision and other issues relating to the performance of the tasks for the purpose for which it was founded;
- through the work of Supervisory Board of HRT, which has a task to control and monitor spending of funds;
- with the provision of quality public service, that is agreed upon through public discussion and conducted 'test of public value';
- by the conclusion of the Contract between Croatian Radio-Television and the Government of Republic of Croatia (Contract) that regulates in more detail the part of the HRT's mandate relating to the content of the programmes, their objectives, duration and source and amount of funds for financing of HRT.

153. Article 17 of the CRTA stipulates that HRT is independent in its activity. Its independence is reflected mainly through HRT's editorial independence with regard to programmes, especially in planning, production and determination of the programme schedule. Furthermore, the independence of HRT is also reflected in its right to regulate, through the competence of its bodies and in accordance with the CRTA, its internal organization and the manner of work and its right to, by its general acts, regulate the issues of receiving employees to work, as well as their rights and obligations, in accordance with the law and collective agreements.

253. Article 10 of the CRTA.
254. Article 11(1) of the CRTA.

§2. THE ORGANIZATION OF PUBLIC SERVICE BROADCASTING

I. National Public Service Broadcaster: Croatian Radio-Television (HRT)

154. Croatian Radio-Television (HRT) is the national public service broadcaster, who creates, produces and broadcasts the following:

- four national television channels (*HTV1*, *HTV2*, *HTV3* and *HTV4*);
- eight regional TV centres;
- three national radio channels (*HR1*, *HR2* and *HR3*);
- eight regional radio channels;
- one satellite TV channel broadcasting in Croatian;
- two international programmes, the 'Voice of Croatia' on radio and a programme for Croatian diaspora on television;
- an on-demand audiovisual media platform (*HRTi*);
- teletext, Internet and mobile portals.

155. HRT is a full member of the EBU. It has four organizational units (Program, Production, Technology and Business Activity), and one autonomous unit (Support) for administrative and other activities.

156. The two national television channels of HRT are specialized channels. *HTV3* is a TV channel intended to provide cultural, educational, scientific, musical, film and other arts programmes, while *HTV4* is a TV channel specialized in news content.

II. Main Organs of the National Public Service Broadcaster (HRT)

157. According to Article 18 of the CRTA, the main bodies of HRT are: the General Manager of HRT; the Management Board of HRT; the Supervisory Board of HRT; and the Programme Council of HRT.

A. General Manager of HRT

158. The General Manager of HRT represents and acts on behalf of HRT and is responsible for the legality of business activities of HRT in accordance with the CRTA, the Statute of HRT[255] as well as other rules and regulations. He or she is also responsible for the successful realization of the main goals of HRT, the financial activity of HRT and the realization of the programme principles of HRT. For his/her business activities the General Manager of HRT answers to the Supervisory Board of HRT.[256]

255. Statute of Croatian Radio-Television, December 2012, available at: http://www.hrt.hr/fileadmin/video/Statut_HRT-a.pdf (14 May 2017).
256. Article 19a of the CRTA.

159. According to Article 20 of the CRTA, the General Manager of HRT is appointed and dismissed by the Croatian Parliament. An invitation to public tender for the position of General Manager of HRT is published by the Supervisory Board of HRT. This board determines the list of candidates whose applications are valid and submits the list to the Croatian Parliament's *Committee on Information, Computerisation and the Media*. In their application, candidates must propose the programme of activities and management of HRT for a period of five years. The Committee on Information, Computerisation and the Media then conducts interviews with candidates and proposes the appointment of the best candidate to the Croatian Parliament. The Parliament appoints a General Manager of HRT by majority vote. The mandate of General Manager of HRT lasts for five years.

160. The person who is appointed General Manager must be a Croatian citizen, must have a university degree, active knowledge of one foreign language, ten years of work experience in the field of media or other businesses and knowledge of media legislation and information technologies. Furthermore, the position of General Manager of HRT is disparate with functions in government bodies, local or regional government or bodies of political parties.[257]

161. Article 21 of the CRTA stipulates that the General Manager of HRT:

- manages HRT;
- disposes of assets of HRT, in accordance with the law and Statute of HRT;
- proposes the Statute of HRT to the Supervisory Board;
- proposes a work programme to the Supervisory Board;
- appoints one person from the Management Board as a Deputy General Manager;
- determines the draft of a Contract between HRT and the Croatian government for obligations and financing of HRT;
- proposes a financial plan and annual calculation;
- based on public tender and opinion of journalists and other employees that participate in the creation of HRT programmes, appoints editors in chief;
- drafts the internal acts and materials needed by the Programme Council and Supervisory Board for their work;
- submits an annual report to Supervisory Board and Programme Council;
- submits an annual report to Croatian Parliament;
- performs other activities as well, in accordance with the law and the Statute of HRT.

162. Before the expiration of the term he or she was appointed to, the General Manager of HRT can be dismissed by Croatian Parliament in case should he/she request so himself/herself, should Supervisory Board determine that he/she is not acting in accordance with CRTA and other regulations and Statute of HRT, should he/she unfoundedly refuse to execute the decisions of the Supervisory Board of HRT, should he/she cause serious damages to the HRT by his/her unconscientious and improper work, should he/she fail to execute the annual work programme of

257. Article 20 of the CRTA.

HRT, should he/she fail to execute the Contract between the Croatian government and HRT or in other cases as provided by the CRTA and Statute of HRT.[258]

B. Management Board of HRT

163. The Management Board of HRT consists of the General Manager of HRT and the managers of organizational units (Programme, Production, Technology and Business Activity) determined by Article 22, paragraph 2 of the Statute of HRT. The activities of the Management Board are managed by the General Manager.

164. According to Article 17 of the Statute of HRT, the Management Board of HRT adopts: an Ordinance on internal organization and systematization of jobs; an Ordinance on financial activities of HRT; an Ordinance on protection at work and fire protection; and general terms, as well as a price list, for compensation of external associates. Furthermore, when the Supervisory board of HRT requests it, the Management Board rectifies irregularities in business activities of its members or in the implementation of programme principles of HRT and the contractual obligations for each organizational unit of HRT.

C. Supervisory Board of HRT

165. The Supervisory Board of HRT has five members. Four members of Supervisory Board are appointed and dismissed by the Croatian Parliament with a majority vote. Candidates are selected and nominated by the Committee on Information, Computerisation and the Media, based on public tender. One member of a Supervisory Board is an 'HRT workers' representative' and is appointed in accordance with the CRTA and the Croatian Labour Act. Members of the Supervisory Board elect their president and vice president among themselves and their mandate is four years.[259]

166. Appointed persons must have Croatian citizenship, must have a university degree, active knowledge of one foreign language and have ten years of work experience. When electing members of the Supervisory Board, it is advisable that at least one of the members is from the legal and financial profession and that most of them have work experience in the field of media. They must be appointed at least thirty days before current members' mandate expire.[260]

167. The main tasks of the Supervisory Board of HRT are regulated by Article 23 of the CRTA. More important tasks are:

– adopting the Statute of HRT proposed by General Manager of HRT;

258. Article 20(6) of the CRTA.
259. Article 22 of the CRTA.
260. Article 22(2) of the CRTA.

- supervising the business activities of HRT as lawful and compliant with CRTA provisions that regulate the use of HRT's income;
- the initiation of the procedure to relieve the General Manager of HRT in case that he/she is not acting in accordance with the CRTA, the Statute of HRT or other regulations;
- adopting the work programme of HRT proposed by General Manager of HRT;
- providing an opinion on Contract between the Croatian government and HRT;
- adopting a financial plan, as well as its amendments and annual calculation;
- consenting to the disposition of HRT's financial assets and properties that have a value more than the limit determined by the HRT's Statute, as well as consenting to the conclusion of loan agreements and agreements for legal representation of HRT;
- determining the level of the licence fee in accordance with Article 35 paragraph 2 of the CRTA;
- submitting an annual report about their work to Croatian Parliament.

168. Article 28, paragraph 8 of the CRTA stipulates that a Member of Supervisory Board of HRT can be dismissed by the Croatian Parliament before the end of his/her mandate, in case should he/she request so himself, should it be determined that he/she is not acting in accordance with rules and regulations relevant to activities of HRT, should he/she be absent without a valid reason for more than two consecutive board meetings or within a period of one year, should he/she try to influence the publication of certain programmes, or should he/she, by his/her work or conduct impair the reputation of HRT.

D. Programme Council of HRT

169. The Programme Council of HRT (Council of HRT) is a main advisory body created in the context of public service broadcasting in Croatia to involve various groups of society. According to Article 24 of the CRTA, the Council of HRT represents and protects the interests of the public through supervision and improvement of radio and audiovisual programmes as well as other audio and audiovisual multimedia services.

170. Article 25 of the CRTA stipulates that the Council of HRT has eleven members. Nine of them are appointed and dismissed by the Croatian Parliament. Public tender is published and candidates are selected by the Committee on Information, Computerisation and the Media of the Croatian Parliament. The Committee submits a list of selected candidates to Parliament. The Croatian Parliament then votes on each candidate individually, and the candidates with the highest number of votes are elected. If candidates have an equal number of votes, voting in Parliament is repeated until members of the Council of HRT are appointed. Two members are appointed and dismissed by journalists and other employees of HRT that participate in the creation of programmes as regulated by the CRTA and the Statute of HRT.

171. The public tender that is published by Committee for the appointment of nine members of the Council of HRT calls upon institutions, associations and citizens to nominate their candidates. They must be Croatian citizens and domiciled in Croatia. They must also either be a media or audiovisual works expert, a respected intellectual, established artist, an expert in some other field or another public employee who has proven during the course of his/her career to uphold the highest democratic principles and respect the rule of law. Furthermore, candidates must be prominent in promoting the constitutional values of the Republic of Croatia, the development of civil society, human rights and freedoms, culture, science and arts as well as media freedoms. Selected candidates must represent the different groups of society, the diversity of views and the pluralism of Croatian society.[261]

172. Members of the Council of HRT can't be State officials or persons that carry out duties within a political party, nor local or regional government. Furthermore, members of the Council of HRT may not be employed or performing any other activity in rival firms, i.e., firms performing the activity of production, provision or broadcasting of audio or audiovisual media services, multimedia content, electronic publications. Neither can the members be part of their management or supervisory boards, their shareholders, owners, co-owners or performing any other tasks which could cause a conflict of interests. Members of the Council of HRT, during their mandate, can't have any business or financial arrangement with HRT or be intermediate on behalf of third parties.[262]

173. Article 26 of the CRTA stipulates that the Council of HRT shall:

- monitor, evaluate and supervise the implementation of programme principles and obligations that are determined by the Contract between the Croatian government and HRT (set out in Article 13. CRTA). In case of infringement it will, in written form, notify the Management Board of HRT, the editors in chief and the Supervisory Board of HRT;
- govern the procedure of determining the content of programme obligations of HRT and public discussion about those obligations (set out in Article 13 paragraph 3 of the CRTA) proposed by Management Board of HRT with the consent of EMC;
- give its prior opinion on the proposal of the work programme of HRT;
- give its prior opinion on the proposal of the Contract between the Croatian government and HRT (set out in Article 13. CRTA);
- appoint a commissioner for users of HRT services;
- adopt rules of procedure for its work;
- perform other tasks in accordance with the CRTA and the Statute of HRT.

261. Article 25(2) of the CRTA.
262. Article 25(6) of the CRTA.

174. To guarantee editorial and journalistic independence, the Council of HRT can't view or listen to HRT's programmes or parts of those programmes prior to their broadcast and can't make a decision that would influence publishing of certain programmes.[263]

175. According to Article 27 of the CRTA, a member of the Council of HRT can be dismissed before the expiration of the term he/she was appointed to in case he or she should: request so; give false information during the procedure for appointment; become an employee of a rival firm; become State official; carry out duties within political party or local and regional government; act contrary to the provisions of the CRTA and other legislation; be absent without a valid reason for more than six months from Council meetings; try to influence the publication of certain programmes; or, with his/her actions, undermine the reputation of HRT. The dismissal procedure is initiated by the Council of HRT or the Supervisory Board of HRT, and the final decision is carried out by the Croatian Parliament. In the case of two council members appointed by journalist and employees of HRT, a decision is carried out also by journalist and employees of HRT.

176. The work of the Council of HRT is public. The Council appoints the president from among its members. Decisions are carried out with a majority vote (of all members of the Council). During Council meetings, the General Manager of HRT, president of Supervisory Board of HRT, the editors in chief or other persons invited by the president of the Council can be present but without a right to vote.[264]

177. The Council of HRT appoints a commissioner for users of HRT services. It receives complaints and suggestions from viewers, listeners and other users of HRT services. The commissioner submits a report twice a year to the Council of HRT. A commissioner is the person who fulfils the same terms as for appointment of a member of Council of HRT. His/her mandate lasts for four years. He/she can't be a member of the Council of HRT or the Supervisory Board of HRT.[265]

§3. The Financing of Public Service Broadcasting

178. The regular activities of the national public service broadcaster – HRT are financed from public and commercial revenues. *Public revenue* comprises a monthly licence fee, any (commercial) activities revenue that is considered to be public revenue, revenue from the State budget and revenue from EU funds. *Commercial revenue* comprises funds acquired from commercial activities and all other activities that are not considered public activities.[266] Revenue realized from commercial activities such as broadcasting of audiovisual commercial communications,

263. Article 26(3) of the CRTA.
264. Article 28, Article 31 of the CRTA.
265. Article 32 of the CRTA.
266. Article 38 of the CRTA.

advertising, sponsorship, televoting, sale of radio and audiovisual programmes, sale of tickets for concerts and music services are considered as *public revenue*.[267]

179. Licence fee revenue constitutes State Aid that is used in accordance with State Aid rules and regulations in the public service broadcasting. Thus, Article 13 of the CRTA stipulates that programme obligations of HRT (Articles 9, 10, 11, 12 of the CRTA) and amount and source of revenue for their financing is regulated by the Contract between Croatian Radio-Television and Government of Republic of Croatia. The said Contract comprises type, scope and content of all public services that HRT provides according to CRTA and is concluded for the period of five years.[268]

180. The amount of public compensation for public service broadcasting that is defined by above-mentioned Contract can't be more than the net cost of performing public service broadcasting activities, including all direct or indirect income realized by performing those activities. When determining the net cost of activities, all commercial activities connected to public service broadcasting are taken into account. HRT must draw up a proposal of programme obligations that are part of the Contract and conduct a public discussion on that proposal. HRT must propose the draft of the Contract to the Croatian government six months before the existing Contract expires. Furthermore, for every new radio or television channel or for every new provision of audio and audiovisual media service on-demand or new satellite, Internet, cable or other forms of transmissions, HRT needs permission from the Electronic Media Council of the Republic of Croatia (EMC).[269] HRT can withhold 10% of earnings that are above the net cost of performing public service broadcasting (except in certain cases provided by CRTA in Article 39) and rest of the earnings must be paid to the special account of Croatian EMC. In the following year, those earnings are then paid back to HRT for performing public service broadcasting.[270]

181. The Contract includes qualitative demands for public services provided by HRT for a period of five years, including radio and television channels, their type, purpose and programme basis, number, type and content of Internet portals of HRT, conditions for the provision of other public services, taking into account public needs and development of technology in regards to electronic media. Furthermore, the Contract regulates programme obligations, additional obligations concerning international content broadcasting, programmes for minorities, obligations to inform the public in emergency situations, promotion of public values, music production, technological development of HRT, public value test, financing of strategic projects of HRT, inclusion of sports events in HRT's broadcasting, other online services like

267. Article 38 of the CRTA and Article 91. The Contract between Croatian Radio-Television and Government of Republic of Croatia for the period 2013–2017.
268. Article 13 of the CRTA.
269. *Ibid.*
270. Article 39(3) of the CRTA.

ringtones, real estate advertising, gambling, e-banking, online auctions, platforms for photo, music and video sharing, and other forms of advertising.

182. Public values that are represented and promoted by HRT, as a public service broadcaster in its programmes and services, must be inline and pass the public value test in accordance with basic principles of:

- *universality* – which includes: protection and improvement of general public values, public service that is accessible by everyone, action and interests in public domain, media service that is reference for public, informing and incitement to public engagement in democratic process, provision of public media content across all relevant platforms, interactivity and better connection with public, be an integral part of society, recognition of public service;
- *independence* – which includes: independence from political and commercial influence, functioning within a legal framework that ensures independent and stable public media service, impartiality, active promotion of freedom of speech, right to be informed, responsibility to the public, ensuring editorial independence;
- *excellence and innovation* – which includes: provision of content and service of highest quality, achievement of highest standards, reliability of content and services, competence of staff, incitement of permanent education, incitement of creativity, integrity of media institution, setting of industry benchmark, fostering talents, innovation, taking risks related to creativity.
- *diversity* – which includes: respecting diversity in any way, plurality of views, cross-cultural dialogue, tolerance, programmes and services for persons with specific needs, diversification of kind of programmes;
- *accountability to the public* – which includes: openness, transparency, adequate management, efficiency, dedication to the mission.

183. The Contract defines financing of public services of HRT, structured by year and source, with an overview of costs by year and type, including powers and obligations of HRT bodies in relation to the management of funds for the realization of Contract.[271]

Table 2 Planned Calculations of Earnings and Losses for the Period 2013–2017 in HRK (Article 104 of the Contract Between Croatian Radio-Television and Government of Republic of Croatia for the Period 2013–2017)

	Type	*2013*	*2014*	*2015*	*2016*	*2017*
1	**INCOME**	**1,392,000,000**	**1,407,000,000**	**1,421,000,000**	**1,432,000,000**	**1,441,000,000**
1.1	Licence fee	1,190,000,000	1,205,000,000	1,215,000,000	1,225,000,000	1,235,000,000
1.2	Advertising	111,000,000	111,000,000	115,000,000	115,000,000	115,000,000
1.3	Other income	91,000,000	91,000,000	91,000,000	91,000,000	91,000,000

271. Article 14 of the CRTA.

	Type	*2013*	*2014*	*2015*	*2016*	*2017*
2	**EXPENDITURE**	**1,404,275,344**	**1,406,386,634**	**1,418,366,552**	**1,427,841,680**	**1,437,941,110**
	EARNINGS/ LOSSES	**-12,275,344**	**613,366**	**2,633,448**	**3,158,320**	**3,058,890**

184. Based on the Contract, each year HRT must adopt a working programme and a financial plan for the following year, in which it will determine activities, programme obligations and the required financial means for their realization.[272]

I. Licence Fee

185. The licence fee represents the main source of income for HRT. Every owner or possessor of a radio or television set (or another device that can receive radio or audiovisual programme) must pay a licence fee directly to HRT. Households that have more than one receiver are only required to pay one licence fee. Furthermore, natural persons who are not paying a licence fee for the household must pay a licence fee if they have a receiver in their car. Legal persons pay a license fee for each receiver that they own or possess, with exception of hospitality services, which can use three receivers on one licence fee.[273] Preschools, elementary schools and high schools are exempt from paying a licence fee.[274]

186. Article 35 of the CRTA stipulates that the maximal cost of licence fee may amount to 1.5% of the average monthly net salary of employees in Croatia,[275] based on statistical data for a previous year. The cost of the licence fee for each year is determined by the Supervisory board of HRT, with prior approval of the EMC and in accordance with Article 13 of the CRTA. 3% of the collected monthly revenue from licence fees go to the fund for the promotion of pluralism and diversity of electronic media and 2% of revenue goes to the Croatian Audiovisual Centre (HAVC) for promoting and funding the Croatian film industry.

187. In accordance with Article 38 of the CRTA, the cost of the licence fee (HRK 80) is allocated as follows:

- HRK 55 (68.4%) to the production of programmes;
- HRK 9 (11.7%) to broadcasting, including payments to *Odašiljači i veze* (the infrastructure operator), and the associations for collective rights management (HDS, HUZIP, ZAPRAF);
- HRK 3.5 (4.5%) to the Fund for the promotion of pluralism and diversity of electronic media;
- HRK 3.5 (4.4%) to the expenditures for activities of organizational units of HRT;
- HRK 9 (11%) to business expenses.

272. Article 13(6) of the CRTA.
273. Article 34 of the CRTA.
274. Article 36(3) of the CRTA.
275. In 2016 cost of the license fee was HRK 80.

188. HRT is obligated to monitor direct and indirect income and any expenditure related to public service broadcasting and have separate internal accounting for activities of public service broadcasting and commercial activities.[276] HRT can't use revenue from licence fees or other public income to finance its commercial activities.

II. Commercial Communications on PSB

189. Broadcasting of commercial communications on HRT is regulated by Article 37 of the CRTA. The duration of commercial communications on each radio channel of HRT can't be more than nine minutes in one hour. The duration of commercial communications on each general television channel (*HTV1* and *HTV2)* can't be more than nine minutes in one hour of the programme, while from 18:00 to 22:00 it can't be more than four minutes in one hour of the programme. That does not include announcements of programmes. Broadcasting of commercial communications on specialized television channels (*HTV3* and *HTV4*) is not allowed.[277]

190. Furthermore, teleshopping is forbidden and the broadcasting of movies can be interrupted by commercial communications only once. Journalists, editors and other persons who appear in a news programme are not allowed to participate in any form of commercial communications.[278]

III. Commercial Activities of PSB

191. HRT must conduct its commercial activities in accordance with the rules and regulations on market competition. The price list of marketing services of HRT must not prevent, distort or limit fair market competition. Especially, HRT shall not lower the prices of advertising and other commercial services below the regular market prices and bid for rights for sporting events above market prices.[279] In case of acquisition of audio and audiovisual content of significant value based on exclusive rights, HRT must relinquish unused rights to other broadcasters of radio and television and providers of media services.[280]

IV. Supervising Position of the Electronic Media Council

192. As an independent regulator, EMC supervises the enforcement of provisions of the CRTA and the Contract between Croatian Radio-Television and Government of Republic of Croatia (Article 13 of the CRTA). This includes supervision

276. Article 38(7) of the CRTA.
277. Article 37 of the CRTA.
278. Article 37(8) of the CRTA.
279. Article 40 of the CRTA.
280. Article 40(3) of the CRTA.

over the implementation of programme obligations that are part of the public service of HRT, the decision procedure on the introduction of significantly new audiovisual services, and the issuance of authorizations to start a new radio or television channel or provide new audio and audiovisual media services on-demand, new satellite, Internet, cable, or other new forms of broadcasting of audio and audiovisual programme. It also includes oversight over the usage of revenues from licence fees and other public revenue in accordance with rules and regulations of State Aid for public broadcasting services.[281]

193. For supervision purposes over this usage of revenue from licence fee and other public revenue of HRT, HRT must submit financial reports to the EMC every six months, or whenever such is requested by the EMC.[282]

281. Article 44(1) of the CRTA.
282. Article 44(3) of the CRTA.

Chapter 2. Private Broadcasting

§1. Different Categories of Private Broadcasters

194. In the Republic of Croatia, there are television and radio stations that are broadcasting their programme on a local, regional and national level but there is no specific regulation differentiating local, regional or national broadcasters with regards to their programme. Categories of private broadcasters are primarily defined by the type of license that is awarded to them and means of transmission that is used, where a territorial dimension is defined through the coverage range of allocated frequencies.

I. Categories of Media Service Providers

195. The EMA uses one broad term, *media service providers,* to define various types of broadcasters of different categories of media services (including public service broadcaster since most of the provisions of EMA also apply to PSB). Article 2, paragraph 8 of the EMA defines a media service provider as the natural or legal person who has editorial responsibility for the choice of the content of the audio or audiovisual media service and determines the manner in which it is organized.

196. Different categories of media services that are provided by media service providers are:

- television broadcast (linear audiovisual media service);
- radio broadcast;
- on-demand audiovisual media service (non-linear audiovisual media service);
- near video-on-demand audiovisual media service;
- radio-on-demand media service;
- protected service;
- non-profit audiovisual and/or radio programme services.

197. Pursuant Article 11 of the EMA, all audiovisual media service providers must permanently and directly provide identification information to the users. That information must include the name of the media service provider, the geographical address at which the media service provider is established, the details of the media service provider, including its electronic mail address or website, which allows rapid, direct and efficient contact with the provider, and the competent regulatory and/or supervisory bodies.

II. Television and Radio Broadcasters

198. In the EMA *linear audiovisual media services* are defined as television media services or television broadcasts provided by a media service provider for simultaneous viewing of programmes on the basis of a programme schedule.[283] A media service provider of those television broadcasts (linear audiovisual media services) is referred to as *television broadcaster*.[284] It should be noted that despite the use of the term 'television', this definition also refers to live streaming, webcasting, near-video-on-demand or any other service that is provided regardless of the platform of distribution and on the basis of a programme schedule as linear audiovisual media services. EMA has no specific provision that regulates webcasting or simulcasting, and *near-video-on-demand* is defined separately as an audiovisual media service provided by a media service provider for the viewing of programmes at the moment chosen by the user and at his individual request on the basis of a programme schedule.[285]

199. In accordance with Article 22 of the EMA, the activity of providing television and radio media services may be performed by a legal or natural person (television and radio broadcaster) entered in the court register or other register prescribed in the Republic of Croatia in accordance with the EMA and separate regulation, and which has obtained a concession and concluded a concession contract in accordance with the EMA and the Concessions Act. For the provision of those activities, in addition to the general and programme conditions set out in EMA, a television and radio broadcaster must meet special technical, spatial, financial and personnel conditions. Those conditions are stipulated by the Ordinance on minimum standards for conducting audio and audiovisual media services and for maintaining the register.[286]

200. *Radio broadcaster* is defined as media service provider of radio broadcasts where *radio media service* is defined as the initial transmission and/or publication of the radio programmes intended for reception by the public, by wire or over the air, including that by satellite, in encoded or unencoded form. The term includes the forms of mutual mediation or exchange of radio programmes between radio media service providers with a view to their being relayed to the public.[287]

III. On-Demand Audiovisual Media Services

201. The implementation of two-tier regulation and the introduction of on-demand audiovisual media services in the Croatian regulatory framework for electronic media required a revision of the EMA in 2009. With the transposition of

283. Article 2(11) of the EMA.
284. Article 2(9) of the EMA.
285. Article 2(13) of the EMA.
286. Ordinance on minimum standards for conducting audio and audiovisual media services and maintaining the register, Official Gazette [OG] No. 83/2014.
287. Article 2(22) of the EMA.

AVMSD,[288] provisions were incorporated in the EMA are almost identical to provisions from the AVMSD. In Article 2, paragraph 12 of the EMA, *on-demand audiovisual media services* are defined as audiovisual media services provided by a media service provider for the viewing of programmes at a moment chosen by the user and at his individual request on the basis of a catalogue of programmes selected by the media service provider.

202. Article 2, paragraph 23 of the EMA defines radio-on-demand media service as radio media service provided by a media service provider for the listening of programmes at the moment chosen by the user at his individual request on the basis of a catalogue of programmes selected by the media service provider.

IV. Protected Services

203. Protected services are audiovisual media services as well as information society services where provided against remuneration and on the basis of conditional access, or the provision of conditional access itself to the above-mentioned services. It is assumed that information society service is any service normally provided for remuneration, at a distance, by electronic means and at the individual request of a recipient of services.[289]

204. Article 50 of the EMA stipulates that it is prohibited to manufacture, produce, import, distribute, sell, rent or possess for commercial purposes illicit devices which enable free access to protected services. Installation, maintenance, replacement, advertising or product placement of such devices is also prohibited. Service providers may exercise their right to legal protection and seek damages from the person who violated their rights to the provision of protected services according to the general regulations on damage compensation.[290]

V. Non-profit Audiovisual and Radio Programme Services

205. Non-profit media service providers may be non-profit television and/or radio broadcasters, non-profit media service providers of audiovisual media services on-demand, non-profit media service providers who use satellite, Internet and cable transmission for audiovisual and/or radio programmes and non-profit electronic publications providers.[291]

---

288. Directive 2010/13/EU of the European Parliament and of the Council of 10 March 2010 on the coordination of certain provisions laid down by law, regulation or administrative action in Member States concerning the provision of audiovisual media services (Audiovisual Media Services Directive), OJ L 95, 15.4.2010, pp. 1–24.
289. Article 2(25) of the EMA.
290. Article 51 of the EMA.
291. Article 48 of the EMA.

206. Non-profit media service providers can be institutions, councils and associations of national minorities, educational, healthcare and other institutions, religious communities, student organizations, school associations, civic associations and other non-governmental organizations with legal personality as well as non-profit cooperatives dedicated to meeting the informational, educational, scientific, professional, artistic, cultural, religious and other public needs.

207. Those media service providers must use their profit from broadcasting activities only for the improvement and development of their own activities. Salaries and compensations of employees and members of managerial and supervisory bodies may not exceed the amount obtained by multiplying the largest coefficient of the complexity of jobs of type I and the basis for calculating the salary according to the Act regulating the salaries in the public service and subordinate legislation which establishes coefficients of complexity of jobs in the field of culture.[292]

208. In the Republic of Croatia, salaries for the employees in the public service are determined by a combination of several factors. The salaries of employees in public services are determined by a coefficient system, i.e., grades/positions are linked to task complexity coefficients; the multiplier (salaries calculation base) is fixed every year. Act on salaries in public service[293] determines basic principles. Article 6 of that Act stipulates the type of jobs according to the level of professional qualifications. Type 1 is for the jobs where university qualifications/education or college education is needed. Type 2 is for the jobs where two-year post-secondary school qualifications are needed. Type 3 is for the jobs where secondary school qualification is needed and type 4 is for the jobs where no specific qualifications are needed. Article 7 of the same Act also determines the range of the coefficient for each type of the job, where for the type 1 the range is between 1.05 and 3.50. Civil Service Job Titles and Job Complexity Coefficients Regulation[294] determines the exact coefficient for every job title (e.g., commissary of Croatian National Theatre can have a coefficient of 3,395). Finally, the basis for calculation of salaries is determined by the Government of the Republic of Croatia in the 'Decision on basis for salaries in public service'[295] (for 2017 gross amount was HRK 5,315.24).

209. The non-profit media service provider may broadcast promotional messages for up to three minutes per hour. Provisions of the EMA that regulate commercial communications, sponsorship, product placement, advertising and teleshopping are also adequately applied to the non-profit electronic publications providers.

---

292. Article 48(3) of the EMA.
293. Act on salaries in public service, Official Gazette [OG] No. 27/01, 39/09.
294. Civil Service Job Titles and Job Complexity Coefficients Regulation Official Gazette [OG] No. 25/13, 72/13,151/13, 09/14, 40/14, 51/14, 77/14, 83/14 – Correction 87/14, 120/14, 147/14, 151/14, 11/15, 32/15, 38/15, 60/15, 83/15, 112/15, 122/15, 10/17, 39/17, 40/17 – Correction, 74/17, 122/17).
295. Decision on basis for salaries in public service, Official Gazette [OG] No. 87/2017.

210. Educational institutions or student associations with legal personality may also be considered a non-profit television and/or radio media service provider. Their programmes must be produced and broadcast by students and pupils primarily, and they must be intended for the school and student population. The activity must be performed exclusively as a non-profit radio or television programme. Those programmes must include information of all kinds and author's works whose purpose is to inform and satisfy educational, scientific, professional, artistic, cultural and other needs of children, youth, students and the wider public.[296]

211. The status of the non-profit broadcaster for educational institutions or student associations with legal personality is determined by the EMC in compliance with the EMA when awarding or terminating the concession.[297]

VI. Radio and Television Networks

212. Article 47 of the EMA provides that the broadcasters of television and radio channels may, upon the prior consent of the EMC, integrate into *regional or national networks* covering regional or wider areas. A national network is an audiovisual or radio programme that can be reached by more than 60% of the population of the Republic of Croatia and regional network of programmes is a network accessible to more than 70% of the population in the certain region. After integration, a regional or national network, shall in the sense of programme requirements and limitations set out in the EMA, be considered as a unique audiovisual or radio programme.

213. Conditions for integration in terms of programmes into regional or national networks are as follows:

- networked television and/or radio broadcasters, by a special legal Act, should appoint a responsible editor of the joint programme who will be responsible for the broadcast of audiovisual and/or radio programmes in compliance with the EMA, and forward the legal Act on the appointment to the EMC, within fifteen days prior to the beginning of broadcasting of the joint audiovisual and/or radio programme;
- each of the networked broadcasters should broadcast at least two hours of private production in the area for which they were granted the radio concession, each day, between seven and twenty-two hours;
- the joint private production of networked television and/or radio broadcasters should be produced in the Croatian language, excluding the programmes for the previously mentioned obligations, and should amount to at least 25% of the audiovisual and/or radio programmes broadcast via the network, on a daily basis;

296. Article 49 of the EMA.
297. Article 49 of the (3) EMA.

- the networked television and/or radio broadcasters should create a joint programme basis and written Act on the manner of performing the programme basis, and forward both documents to the EMC, in order to acquire prior consent.

VII. Electronic Publications

214. Besides audio and audiovisual media services, the EMA also regulates electronic publications as a form of electronic media. In Article 2, paragraph 2 of the EMA electronic publications are defined as edited programme contents which the electronic publications providers broadcast daily or periodically via the Internet with a view to providing public information and education. The intention of this provision is to regulate all Internet web pages and Internet portals of registered media publishers, such as Internet portals of newspapers publishers, television broadcasters, radio broadcasters or other information society services that are registered as media publishers and publish media content daily or periodically to provide public information on the Internet.

215. Article 80 of the EMA regulates which provisions of the EMA, pertaining to audiovisual media services, shall be adequately applied to electronic publications. Those provisions are:

- Article 12 of the EMA – the prohibition of services that are jeopardizing the constitutional order and national security; the prohibition to promote, favour the promotion of and spreading of hatred or discrimination based on race or ethnic affiliation or colour, gender, language, religion, political or other belief, national or social origin, property, trade union membership, education, social status, marital or family status, age, health condition, disability, genetic heritage, native identity, expression or sexual orientation, as well as the prohibition of anti-Semitism and xenophobia, and the ideas of the fascist, nationalist, communist and other totalitarian regimes; prohibited is also the publishing of information revealing the identity of a child up to 18 years of age involved in cases of any type of violence, regardless of the child's status as witness, victim or perpetrator, or in cases of attempted suicide or committed suicide, as well as to introduce details of a child's family affairs and private life.
- Article 15 of the EMA – the obligation to broadcast emergency announcements free of charge.
- Article 26 of the EMA – the prohibition to publish content which offends human dignity, content which especially contains immoral and pornographic content or content that in any manner encourage, promote and glorify violence and crime and encourage citizens, especially children and youth, to use tobacco products, alcohol or drugs. Paragraph 2 of the Article 26 prohibits content that might seriously impair the physical, mental or moral development of minors and paragraph 3 regulates broadcasting of content that is likely to impair the physical, mental or moral development of minors.

– Article 27 of the EMA – the obligation to keep records of the entirety of published content for at least ninety days from the day of its publishing and its delivery to the EMC upon request.

216. The EMA does not recognize the distinction between audiovisual (video) and other content published by electronic publication providers on the Internet. The issue is whether audiovisual parts (video) of an electronic publication should be treated as a separate service, an on-demand audiovisual media service, or whether the service as a whole should be treated as an electronic publication. Examining the current practice of the EMC, it is clear that such mixed media content on the Internet is treated solely as an electronic publication. The EMC does not impose an obligation on electronic publication providers with video content to also register as on-demand audiovisual media providers. Most Croatian online newspapers include video in their publications; sometimes that video is linked from other sources (e.g., YouTube), but sometimes they also include a video that is their own production. Under current rules, such video must be in accordance with Articles 12, 15, 26 and 27.

§2. Licensing Requirements

I. Jurisdiction

217. The activity of broadcasting audiovisual media services (linear and on-demand) and electronic publications in the Republic of Croatia can be performed by media service providers registered in the court register or other register prescribed in the Republic of Croatia, as long as, along with the general conditions, its head office and editorial office are in the Republic of Croatia.[298]

218. Electronic publication provider whose head office is located in another Member State of the EU or another State which is a contracting party to the Agreement on the EEA may permanently publish electronically in the Republic of Croatia if they register in the court registry or other appropriate registry and have an editorial office in the Republic of Croatia.[299] Furthermore, the electronic publication provider whose head office is located in another Member State of the EU or another State which is a contracting party to the Agreement on the EEA may perform the activity of providing electronic publications in the Republic of Croatia on a temporary or occasional basis, in accordance with the provisions of the Services Act.[300]

219. With regards to jurisdiction, Article 6 of the EMA stipulates that audiovisual media service providers under the jurisdiction of the Republic of Croatia are those providers who are established in the Republic of Croatia[301] or those deemed

298. Article 5(1) of the EMA.
299. Article 5(2) of the EMA.
300. Article 5(3) of the EMA.
301. Article 6(1) of the EMA.

to be under the jurisdiction of the Republic of Croatia in case they use a satellite up-link situated in the Republic of Croatia or they do not use a satellite up-link situated in the Republic of Croatia but they use satellite capacity appertaining to the Republic of Croatia. A media service provider shall be deemed to be established in the Republic of Croatia when its head office is located in the Republic of Croatia and the editorial decisions about the audiovisual media services are taken in the Republic of Croatia. Where an audiovisual media service provider has its head office in the Republic of Croatia and where the editorial decisions about the audiovisual media services are taken in another Member State of the EU, or where an audiovisual media service provider has its head office in another Member State of the EU and the editorial decisions about the audiovisual media services are taken in the Republic of Croatia, the audiovisual media service provider shall be deemed to be established in the Republic of Croatia provided that a significant part of the workforce involved in the pursuit of the activities concerning audiovisual media services operates in the Republic of Croatia. In case that significant part of the workforce involved in the pursuit of the activities concerning audiovisual media services operates in the Republic of Croatia or in another Member State of the EU, the media service provider shall be deemed to be established in the Republic of Croatia if its head office is located there. In case that significant part of the workforce involved in the pursuit of the activities concerning audiovisual media services operates in neither the Republic of Croatia nor a Member State of the EU, the media service provider shall be deemed to be established in the Republic of Croatia if this is where it first began its activity in accordance with the Croatian legislation, provided that it maintains a stable and effective link with the Croatian economy. Where an audiovisual media service provider has its head office in the Republic of Croatia, but decisions on audiovisual media services are taken in a non-EU country, or vice versa, it shall be deemed to be established in the Republic of Croatia, provided that a significant part of the workforce involved in the pursuit of the activities concerning audiovisual media services operates in the Republic of Croatia.

220. Media service providers to whom above-mentioned provisions are not applicable shall be deemed to fall under the jurisdiction of the Republic of Croatia in the following cases:

– if they use a satellite up-link situated in the Republic of Croatia; or
– if they do not use a satellite up-link situated in the Republic of Croatia but they use a satellite capacity appertaining to the Republic of Croatia.[302]

221. If the question as to whether a media service provider falls under the jurisdiction of the Republic of Croatia or another Member State of the EU may not be determined in accordance with Article 6 of the EMA, the competent Member State shall be that in which the media service provider is established within the meaning of Articles 48–50 of the Stabilisation and Association Agreement between the Republic of Croatia and European Communities and its Member States.

302. Article 6(7) of the EMA.

II. Award of Concessions for Radio and Television Broadcasting

222. For broadcasting radio and television programmes in analogue and digital technology via the terrestrial network of transmitters, broadcasters (media service providers) must have a concession. The competence to award concessions lies with the Electronic Media Council of the Republic of Croatia (and its Agency) and Croatian Regulatory Authority for Network Industries. The procedure for the award of concessions is defined by the EMA and the Concessions Act[303] and is carried out by the Electronic Media Council.

223. The area of a concession may be at the national, regional, county, city, municipality or other level. A concession at the national level comprises at least 60% of the population of the Republic of Croatia, while a concession at the regional level comprises at least 70% of the population within the region.[304] A concession can be granted for a period of time which may not exceed fifteen years or be shorter than eight years depending on the service provided (television or radio) and the area covered. According to Article 4 of the Ordinance on the content and procedure of the notice of intent on granting concessions for the provision of television and radio media services[305] concessions are granted as follows:

For television broadcasting	
- more than 1,500,000 people	15 years
- from 750,000–1,499,999 people	13 years
- from 500,000–749,999 people	12 years
- less than 499,999	10 years
For radio broadcasting	
- more than 1,500,000 people	15 years
- from 750,000–1,499,999 people	14 years
- from 500,000–749,999 people	13 years
- from 300,000–499,999 people	12 years
- from 100,000–299,999	11 years
- from 50,000–199,999	10 years
- less than 49,999	9 years

224. The EMC carries out preparatory actions for the award of concessions in line with the Concessions Act.[306]

303. Concessions Act, Official Gazette [OG] No. 66/2017.
304. Article 75 of the EMA.
305. Ordinance on the content and procedure of the notice of intent on granting concessions for the provision of television and radio media services, Official Gazette [OG] No. 131/2013.
306. Article 72 of the EMA.

225. Article 73 of the EMA stipulates that the EMC publishes *a notice* of intent to award concessions for the activities of television and radio media service broadcasting on a technical basis, determined by the Croatian Regulatory Authority for Network Industries in accordance with the legislation on electronic communications (ECA). That notice is published for each available radio frequency or more radio frequencies which comprise a single concession, i.e., in the case of digital radio and television for the free transmission capacity of an individual radio or television programme within the multiplex.

226. The procedure to award concessions and the content of the notice of Article 73, paragraph 1 of the EMA is stipulated by the 'EMC Ordinance on the content and procedure of the notice of intent on granting concessions for the provision of television and radio media services'.

227. The main criteria in order to award concessions for the provision of radio and television media services are set out in Article 73 paragraph 4 of the EMA as follows:

- the programme conditions in accordance with EMA, and especially the quantity of own production, European audiovisual works and works of independent producers;
- the time of broadcast;
- the quality and diversity of audiovisual and/or radio programmes;
- the special technical, financial (amount of resources and financial guarantees) and personnel conditions;
- the plan to abide the provisions of EMA and legislation regulating tax and other obligations of legal entities towards the State budget and budget of the units of local and regional self-government, and legal persons in their ownership.

228. A tender based on the published notice must contain evidence on the fulfilment of conditions stipulated by the notice, a programme basis in compliance with the EMA, data on the ownership structure of the legal person submitting the tender, personal data on the company and its head office, i.e., name and family name and permanent residence of persons who directly or indirectly, through other legal persons, have stocks or shares in that legal person, as well as data on the percentage of those stocks or shares. A tender must also contain data on the tenderer's financial capability to perform the activities involved in being television and radio broadcaster.[307]

229. The EMC shall pass *a decision* on the grant of the concession after the conducted procedure of public tender, as well as the procedure of establishing the conditions for granting a concession according to the Concession Act. The decision to

307. Article 73(5) of the EMA.

award the concession contains appropriate data in line with the tender documentation submitted and the provisions of the EMA, the Concessions Act and the Ordinance on the content and procedure of the notice of intent on granting concessions for the provision of television and radio media services.[308]

230. On the basis of a decision on the grant of the concession, the EMC enters into a *concession contract* with the most advantageous tenderer.[309] The concession contract, in addition to the conditions important for the exercise of the concession also contains the *programme basis* and other conditions from the tender for the award of the concession.

231. The right to perform the activities of providing television and radio media service broadcasting is obtained on the basis of the EMC decision granting the concession as well as the contracted concession agreement.[310]

A. *Programme Basis*

232. According to Article 22 of the EMA, the *programme basis* of the television or radio broadcaster, that is part of the concession contract, shall contain a programme scheme determining:
For *general* television or radio broadcasts:

- the type of audiovisual or radio programmes or classification thereof into separate groups;
- the foreseen quantitative ratio among individual content groups;
- the foreseen maximum scope of advertising contents;
- the foreseen scope of its own audio and audiovisual works and the share of the Croatian audio and audiovisual works;
- time of broadcast;
- the proportion of European works;
- the proportion of independent audiovisual works;

For *specialized* television or radio broadcast:

- the type of audiovisual or radio programmes of which over 70% shall be of the same kind;
- the foreseen quantitative ratio among individual content groups;
- the foreseen maximum scope of advertising contents;
- the foreseen scope of its own audio and audiovisual works and the share of the Croatian audio and audiovisual works;
- the proportion of European works;

308. Article 73(7) of the EMA.
309. Article 74 of the EMA.
310. Article 74(1) of the EMA.

- the proportion of independent audiovisual works and other works for the broadcasters of specialized television programme;
- time of broadcast.

233. If a television or radio broadcaster wants to change or make an addition to the programme basis, he is obliged to obtain the prior opinion of the editorial office comprising the editor-in-chief and editors of individual audiovisual or radio programmes. The opinion of the editorial office is established by a majority vote. If a change or addition of programme basis relates to more than 10% of its content, pursuant to which the concession was granted, a broadcaster must also obtain the prior consent of EMC. The programme basis of the television or radio broadcaster pursuant to which the concession was awarded, and its modifications are public and published on the website of the EMC.

B. Time of Broadcasting

234. Article 36 of the EMA stipulates that radio broadcasters at the national and regional level and the level of counties and the city of Zagreb must broadcast at least twelve hours of radio programme per day, and radio broadcasters at a level lower than the county level must broadcast at least six hours of radio programme per day unless the concession contract provides for an extended time.

235. For television broadcasters at the national and regional level and the level of counties and the city of Zagreb, according to Article 36, paragraph 4 of the EMA, there is an obligation to broadcast at least six hours of audiovisual programme per day, and television broadcasters at a level lower than the county level must broadcast at least three hours of audiovisual programme per day, unless the concession contract provides for an extended time.

236. Both television and radio broadcasters at the regional level must reserve at least 10% of their total weekly audio or audiovisual programmes in order to broadcast news and announcements in the concession area unless the concession contract provides for the longer time of broadcast of the news and announcements. Television and radio broadcaster at the local level must reserve at least 10% of their total weekly audio or audiovisual programmes in order to broadcast local news and announcements in the concession area unless the concession contract provides for the longer time of broadcast of the local news and announcements.

237. Television and radio broadcaster at the State and regional level must also broadcast current affairs programme during at least thirty minutes per day, where at least one current affairs show must last at least twenty minutes unless the concession contract provides for an extended amount of time.[311]

311. Article 36(5) of the EMA.

238. Pursuant to Article 27 of the EMA, the television and radio broadcaster must keep a record of the broadcasted audiovisual or radio programme and keep the taped material of the entire broadcast programme for at least ninety days from the day of broadcast. In the event of a complaint or dispute, it is obliged to keep the taped material of the disputed content until the dispute ends. Upon the request of the EMC, the broadcaster must deliver taped material without any delay. The manner of recordkeeping and the quality of the taped material is stipulated by the 'Ordinance on minimum standards for conducting audio and audiovisual media services and maintaining the register'.[312]

C. Transfer, Extension and Register of Concessions

239. A transfer of the concession for radio and television broadcasting is not allowed.[313] The concession fee must be paid to the account of the State Budget. Concessions for the performance of television and radio media services are registered in the register (the book of concessions for the provision of television and/or radio services[314]) administered by the EMC in accordance with Ordinance on the register of providers of media services, electronic publications and producers of non-profit audiovisual and/or radio programmes[315] and concession register that is administered by the Ministry of Finance.

240. Upon request of the television or radio broadcaster EMC may take a decision to award the concession again to the same broadcaster for the following period, by publishing a notice of intent to grant a concession again, if the television or radio broadcaster performs an activity in compliance with the EMA, other relevant regulations as well as the concession contract, and fulfils the criteria stipulated by the 'Ordinance on the content and procedure of the notice of intent on granting concessions for the provision of television and radio media services'. The television or radio broadcaster must submit a request for the renewal of the concession to the EMC at least six months prior to the expiration of the duration of the existing concession.[316]

III. Licence for the Provision of On-Demand Audio and Audiovisual Media Services

241. In accordance with Article 19 of the EMA, on-demand audiovisual media services in the Republic of Croatia can be provided by legal or natural persons in accordance with Articles 5 and 6 of the EMA (establishment and jurisdiction) and

312. Ordinance on minimum standards for conducting audio and audiovisual media services and maintaining the register, Official Gazette [OG] No. 83/2014.
313. Article 74(5) of the EMA.
314. Available at: https://pmu.e-mediji.hr/Public/PregledTvNakladnici.aspx (16 Oct. 2017).
315. Ordinance on the register of providers of media services, electronic publications and producers of non-profit audiovisual and/or radio programmes, Official Gazette [OG] No. 134/2013, 79/2014.
316. Article 78 of the EMA.

has the EMC's licence for providing these activities. For the provision of those services, EMC issues the licence on the basis of the request of the media service provider.

242. The media service provider of on-demand audiovisual media services must fulfil the technical conditions for the transmission of those services and have a programme basis which contains the programme orientation (general or specialized on-demand audiovisual media service).

243. Before deciding on issuing the licence, the EMC is authorized to exchange information about the on-demand media service provider with regulatory bodies of the other Member States of the EU, if its activities are referred also to the other Member States of the EU.

244. The EMC shall decide on the issuance or the non-issuance of the licence as soon as possible, and at the latest within thirty days after receiving the correct request. On the basis of the issuance of the licence, the on-demand media service provider will be registered into the register (the book of on-demand media services providers[317]) administered by the EMC in accordance with the 'Ordinance on the register of providers of media services, electronic publications and producers of non-profit audiovisual and/or radio programmes'.

245. The licence for the provision of on-demand audio and/or audiovisual media services is issued for an unlimited period of time and can be transferred to another person together with the property, rights and obligations essential to the uninterrupted continuance of exercise of the licence, with the prior consent of the EMC.

IV. Licence for Satellite, Internet and Cable Transmission

246. Article 79 of the EMA stipulates that media service providers, who are not obligated under EMA to have a concession for the broadcasting of their programme and are not on-demand audiovisual media services, must also have a licence for the transmission of their programmes. These are all media service providers that use satellite, Internet, cable or other permissible forms of transmission for their programme.

247. The said licence is issued by the EMC, on the basis of a request of the media service provider. Technical conditions for the transmission of programmes, as well as programme basis and principles, must be met.

248. Before deciding on the issuance of the licence, the EMC is authorized to exchange information on the media service provider who requested the licence, with regulatory bodies of the other Member States of the EU, if the transmission of programmes refers to the other Member States of the EU as well.

---

317. Available at: https://pmu.e-mediji.hr/Public/PregledNaZahtjev.aspx (16 Oct. 2017).

249. The EMC shall decide whether it issues or refuses to issue the licence as soon as possible and at the latest within thirty days from receiving the correct request. Based on the issued licence the media service provider is then registered into the register (the book of media service providers of satellite, Internet, cable and other permitted forms of transmission[318]) which is administered by the EMC in accordance with the 'Ordinance on the register of providers of media services, electronic publications and producers of non-profit audiovisual and/or radio programmes'.

250. The licence for satellite, Internet and cable transmission of audiovisual and radio programmes is issued for an unlimited period of time and can be transferred to another person together with the property, rights and obligations essential to the uninterrupted continuance of exercising the licence, with the prior consent of the EMC.

V. Register of Electronic Publications

251. Natural and legal persons (electronic publications providers) must, before their first electronic publication, apply to be registered in the register (the book of electronic publications providers[319]), under the supervision of the EMC. The method of application is determined by the Ordinance on the register of providers of media services, electronic publications and producers of non-profit audiovisual and/or radio programmes.

VI. Temporary or Permanent Withdrawal of Concession or Licence

252. Article 76 of the EMA stipulates that the EMC can temporarily or permanently withdraw *a concession* for television and/or radio broadcasting if it has determined:

- that the concession was awarded on the basis of incorrectly presented data which were important to the selection of the most advantageous tenderer;
- that the television and/or radio broadcaster has not started to exercise the concession within the deadline determined by the concession contract or does not respect the technical conditions of the concession contract for a period longer than one month since the beginning of the exercise of the concession, or stops exercising the concession for a period longer than forty-eight hours;
- that the television and/or radio broadcaster no longer fulfils the requirements to provide the television and/or radio media services, specifically, that such activities may only be performed by legal and natural person entered in the court register or other register prescribed in the Republic of Croatia and which has obtained a concession and concluded a concession contract;

318. Available at: https://pmu.e-mediji.hr/Public/PregledSatelitInternet.aspx (16 Oct. 2017).
319. Available at: https://pmu.e-mediji.hr/Public/PregledElPublikacije.aspx (16 Oct. 2017).

- upon expiration of the period for which it was granted;
- if the media service provider renounces the concession;
- by the cessation of the legal person of a media service provider or the cessation of craft;
- if the media service provider was prohibited by an effective decision of the court to perform an activity for which the concession was awarded;
- by a mutual termination of the concession contract;
- by a permanent termination of a concession.

253. Furthermore, EMC can pass a decision on temporary or permanent withdrawal of *concession or licence* for any media service provider in case that the media service provider:

- performs an activity even after the third warning by the EMC which they issued in the previous twelve months, contrary to the provisions of the EMA and the regulations adopted on the basis of the EMA or to the concession contract;
- publishes audiovisual or radio programmes contrary to the EMA provisions regulating the protection of constitutional order, hate speech and protection of minors (Articles 12, 20 and 26 of the EMA);
- even after receiving a warning from the Council, fails to adhere to a minimum of 90% of the programme basis agreed upon in the procedure of issuing concession or licence;
- even after receiving a warning from the Council, doesn't comply with the established time of broadcasting (Article 36 of the EMA);
- failed to enable the right to short news reports for another media service provider (Article 45 of the EMA);
- failed to pay the concession fee more than twice consecutively or is generally disorderly in paying the concession fee;
- failed to forward information on the change of data, even after receiving a warning by the Council, in accordance with the provision to guarantee publicity of ownership (Article 52 of the EMA);
- is part of an impermissible concentration as determined by provisions of the EMA (Restriction of Concentration – Articles 54–62);
- failed to obtain the approval of the competent association for collective exercise of copyrights and related rights within a determined deadline, even after receiving a warning by the Council;
- transferred the concession to another person;
- transfers the licence to another person contrary to the provisions that regulate the procedure for issuing of the licence for on-demand audiovisual media services or Satellite, Internet and Cable Transmission (Articles 19 and 79 of the EMA);
- regardless of the Council decision on measures for the purpose of temporary limitation of the freedom to broadcast audiovisual media services from other States, publishes audiovisual programmes referred to in Article 77 of the EMA.

254. For media service providers that broadcast audio or audiovisual media services on-demand, via satellite, Internet and cable transmission, EMC will ex officio withdraw the licence and delete the media service provider from the registry of providers of media services, electronic publications and producers of non-profit audiovisual and/or radio programmes, if the media service provider:

- notifies the Council in writing on the cessation of the provider's activity;
- ceases to provide the activities for a period longer than a year;
- no longer fulfils the technical conditions for the transmission of audiovisual and radio programmes;
- was prohibited by an effective decision of the court to perform the registered activity;
- ceases to exist as a legal person or the cessation of craft;[320]
- enters into an impermissible media concentration prescribed by EMA was realized.

320. A craft business is the independent and continuous performance of permitted economic activities by natural persons with the purpose of realizing profits by production, trading of goods or provision of services on the market (Act on Craft Business, Official Gazette No. 143/13). For free crafts, the Act does not require a passed professional qualification or master craftsman exam or any other special professional qualification. Qualified crafts constitute those for which a professional qualification or master craftsman exam must be passed. Privileged crafts are conducted only on the basis of a privilege issued by a competent ministry depending on craft type.

Chapter 3. Programme Standards

§1. General Obligations

255. With the EMA, the Republic of Croatia transposed the AVMSD into Croatian media legislation. The EMA introduced all obligations arising from the AVMSD, such as rules on the identification of media service providers, the prohibition of incitement to hatred, the protection of minors, access to short news extracts, the regulation of events of major importance and the promotion of European works for linear audiovisual media services and for on-demand audiovisual media services. Some of the imposed obligations are imposed as *general obligations* for all media services equally and some specific obligations are imposed for linear audiovisual media services (television broadcasters) and/or on-demand audiovisual media services.

256. General programme obligations that pertain to all media service providers (including electronic publications where applicable) include the following:

- a media service which jeopardizes the constitutional order and national security is not allowed;[321]
- audiovisual media service providers are not allowed to transmit cinematographic works outside periods agreed with the rights holders;[322]
- media service providers are obliged to fairly conduct prize competitions (quiz shows, riddles, etc.) or various forms of reward for the participation of the viewers or listeners in the audiovisual or audio (radio) programmes. They are also obliged to announce the unequivocal rules on this type of content and the public promise of a reward.[323] Conditions for the provision of those services are regulated by the 'Ordinance on the protection of minors in electronic media' (OPM);[324]
- in case of war situations or immediate danger to the independence and integrity of the Republic of Croatia, as well as in case of large natural disasters, technical and technological and ecology disasters and outbreaks, the media service provider is obliged to, upon the request of the competent State body, broadcast announcements free of charge, as well as the official statements by the competent State bodies when there is a danger to people's life and health, the safety of the country or the public order and peace.[325]

257. Other general programme obligations, pertaining to all media services, regarding protection of minors and respect for human dignity are covered in their respective chapters below.

321. Article 12(1) of the EMA.
322. Article 13(1) of the EMA.
323. Article 13(2) of the EMA.
324. Ordinance on the protection of minors in electronic media Official Gazette [OG] No. 28/2015.
325. Article 15 of the EMA.

§2. IMPARTIALITY

258. According to Article 24 of the EMA, audiovisual and radio programmes of television and radio broadcasters must in particular broadcast truthful information, respect human dignity and human rights and fundamental freedoms and contribute to the respect of other people's opinions and beliefs. Their programmes must contribute to the free formation of opinions, to the versatile and objective information of listeners and viewers, as well as to their education and entertainment, to promote Croatian cultural heritage and to encourage listeners and viewers to participate in the cultural life. Furthermore, programmes must promote international understanding and the public's sense of justice, defend democratic freedoms, serve the protection of the environment, fight for the equality of women and men and promote understanding for members of national minorities.

259. Article 25 of the EMA stipulates that broadcasters must present events realistically in their programmes and that different approaches and opinions must be represented. Furthermore, news programmes must be presented truthfully and correctly, presenting facts and events. They must be impartial and professionally correct and they must encourage free forming of opinions. Opinions and comments must be easily recognizable as an opinion or a comment, and it must be obvious whose opinion or comment is being published.

260. In their programmes, all television and radio broadcasters are obliged to promote impartiality, respecting differences in opinions on political or economic issues or with regard to current public policies.

261. Pursuant to Article 28 of the EMA it is forbidden for State bodies and their representatives, as well as labour unions and various interest groups, to exert influence over a television and radio broadcaster with regard to the creation of audiovisual or radio programme.

§3. CULTURAL DIVERSITY

I. Protection of the Croatian Language

A. Use of Croatian Language

262. As a general rule, media service providers founded and registered in the Republic of Croatia must disseminate their programmes in the Croatian language and Latin script or with the translation into the Croatian language.[326]

326. Article 4(1) of the EMA.

263. Media service providers may also promote audio and audiovisual works in the dialects of the Croatian language, which is considered a fulfilment of the obligation to disseminate programmes in the Croatian language.[327]

264. Exemptions to the above-mentioned general rule, where the use of the Croatian language is not obligatory, include:

- if films and other audio and audiovisual works are broadcast in their authentic form;[328]
- if musical works are broadcast with lyrics, which are either partially or fully in a foreign language;
- if broadcasts are either partially or fully intended for the learning of foreign language and script.[329]

265. Furthermore, the use of the Croatian language is not obligatory in broadcasts intended for members of national minorities, or if the media service provider is broadcasting informative programmes or service information for the needs of foreign guests in the languages according to the representation of foreign guests in the area of its concession.[330]

B. Croatian Audiovisual Works

266. Audiovisual works originally produced in the Croatian language or works intended for national minorities in their languages, as well as works of Croatian cultural heritage, are all considered to be Croatian audiovisual works.[331]

267. However, these audiovisual works need to be expressed with pictures which in consecutive order create an impression of motion expressed as individual intellectual creation, such as films and dramas, cultural and artistic and entertaining series, documentary, educational and other audiovisual works.[332]

268. More detailed measures for determining programmes which are considered to be Croatian audiovisual works are stipulated by the Ordinance on Croatian audiovisual works.[333]

269. According to Article 2 of the Ordinance on Croatian audiovisual works, works whose original versions are exclusively, or mainly, in the Croatian language

327. Article 4(2) of the EMA.
328. If foreign films or audiovisual works are originally created in a language that is similar to Croatian language and is intelligible to Croatian citizens there is no need to translate those works (e.g., Serbian or Bosnian and Herzegovinian works).
329. Article 4(3) of the EMA.
330. Article 4(5) of the EMA.
331. Article 40(1) of the EMA.
332. Article 40(2) of the EMA.
333. Ordinance on Croatian audiovisual works, Official Gazette [OG] No. 43/2010.

are deemed to be Croatian audiovisual works, except in justifiable cases where for artistic or other reasons the Croatian language or even speech as such is not used. Pursuant to Article 3 of the Ordinance, works intended for national minorities in their respective languages are also to be deemed Croatian audiovisual works, if original versions of those works are exclusively, or mainly, in the language of the relevant national minority, except in justifiable cases where, for artistic or other reasons, the national minority language or even speech as such is not used.

270. Croatian audiovisual works are also works originating from the Republic of Croatia. Works produced mainly by authors and workers residing in the Republic of Croatia are deemed to be the works originating from Croatia provided that their producers are established or registered in the Republic of Croatia, the production of an individual work is supervised and actually controlled by one or more producers established in the Republic of Croatia, or the contribution of co-producers from the Republic of Croatia to the total co-production costs shall be preponderant and the co-production is not controlled by one or more producers established outside the Republic of Croatia.[334]

271. Croatian audiovisual works are also cinematographic or television feature, documentary, animated, advertising or other films as well as other audiovisual works from the Croatian cultural and artistic production. Furthermore, works mentioned above, which originate, by their content, from literary works, scientific facts, knowledge or achievements, artistic practice or other templates for personal author's realization of an audiovisual work, such as an original scenario and the like, are also considered as Croatian audiovisual works.[335]

272. Programme contents which only directly relate to the areas of literature, science, culture and art so as to inform the public on activities in those areas or to comment on them are not deemed as Croatian audiovisual works. In addition, programme contents which, in live or deferred transmission, transmit a literary, scientific, cultural or artistic event or an author's work are not deemed as Croatian audiovisual works. Furthermore, daily news or other current affairs programmes of an informative character is not considered as Croatian audiovisual works. This does not apply to programme contents which is an expression of an individual intellectual creation of the author of the relevant audiovisual work or when the processing of a transmitted event or author's work significantly surpasses the plain technical character of transmission.[336]

C. Croatian Music

273. Croatian music must comprise at least 20% of the daily broadcast of a music programme, anticipated by the programme scheme in the programme basis

334. Article 4 *Ibid.*
335. Article 5 *Ibid.*
336. Article 6 *Ibid.*

of the radio programme. No more than 20% of the daily broadcast in which Croatian music is performed can be considered for the portion of in-house productions. For specialized radio broadcasting, a quota of 20% does not apply.[337]

II. Content Obligations (Quota)

A. *In-House Production*

274. According to Article 37 of the EMA, in-house production comprises news and current affairs, cultural and artistic, music, sport and other shows and other originally produced audiovisual and radio programmes of which the producer is the television or radio broadcaster or that was produced upon their order and for their account.

275. If several television and radio broadcasters had an input in the production of an audio and audiovisual programme, an in-house production for each of them is considered a part proportional to the input.

276. The premiere and first reruns of Croatian audiovisual works are considered as in-house productions. Advertisements, including radio and television sale and paid information, are not considered as in-house audio or audiovisual programmes.

277. Detailed measurements to determine which programmes should be considered as in-house productions are stipulated by the 'EMC Ordinance on detailed measures for determining audiovisual and/or radio programmes that are considered in-house productions'.[338]

278. In-house productions must amount to at least 20% of the daily time for broadcast of each audiovisual programme of a television broadcaster, of which at least 50% shall be between sixteen and twenty-two hours, except if otherwise stipulated by the EMA.[339]

279. The portion of in-house production must amount to at least 30% of the daily time for broadcast of each radio programme of a radio broadcaster, except if otherwise stipulated by EMA.[340]

280. The rerun of a radio or television show must be clearly marked in line with the technical possibilities. Only the first rerun of a show may be calculated into the in-house production.

---

337. Article 39 of the EMA.
338. Ordinance on detailed measures for determining audiovisual and/or radio programmes that are considered in-house productions, Official Gazette [OG] No. 132/2014.
339. Article 38(1) of the EMA.
340. Article 38(2) of the EMA.

B. European Works

281. Pursuant to Article 41 of the EMA European works means the following:

- works originating in the Member States of the EU;
- works originating in European States party to the European Convention on Transfrontier Television and fulfil the condition that those works are mainly made with authors and workers residing in a Member State of the EU or European States that are party of the European Convention on Transfrontier Television provided that they are made by producers established in one or more of the mentioned States, or production of an individual work is supervised and actually controlled by one or more producers established in one or more of the mentioned States or the contribution of co-producers of the mentioned States to the total co-production costs is preponderant and the co-production is not controlled by one or more producers established outside the mentioned States;
- works co-produced within the framework of agreements related to the audiovisual sector concluded between the EU and third countries and fulfilling the conditions defined in each of those agreements.

282. Works that are not considered European works within the meaning of Article 41 of the EMA, but that are produced within the framework of bilateral co-production treaties concluded between the Member States of the EU and third countries shall be deemed to be European works, provided that the co-producers from the EU supply a majority share of the total cost of the production and that the production is not controlled by one or more producers established outside the territory of the Member States of the EU.

283. Article 42 of the EMA stipulates that television broadcasters must use their best efforts to reserve a majority proportion of their annual transmission time for European works. Broadcasters who cannot attain a majority proportion of their annual transmission time for European works must progressively increase the proportion of European works every year in relation to the past year in accordance with the criteria and the method laid down in the 'Ordinance on the criteria and manner of increasing the share of the European works',[341] taking into account the television broadcaster's informational, educational, cultural and entertainment responsibilities to its viewers, where the minimum initial proportion must be 20% of the annual transmission time.

284. Pursuant to Article 5 of the 'Ordinance on the criteria and manner of increasing the share of the European works', an audiovisual media service provider who is required to increase the share of European works in its programme, in order to achieve a majority share of European works, must successively increase the share by at least 10% each year over a period of the last four years. *Mutatis mutandis*, that also applies to on-demand audiovisual media services.

341. Ordinance on the criteria and manner of increasing the share of the European works, Official Gazette [OG] No. 77/2015.

285. The audiovisual media service providers who have been awarded a concession or permission for satellite, cable and Internet transmission on a programme basis, which contains more than 20% and less than 51% of European works, are required to increase their share over a four-year span.[342]

286. For existing audiovisual media service providers who have received a concession on a national and regional level, these provisions have been applicable since 2008. For all other audiovisual media service providers, the first year of applying the Ordinance provisions is the year subsequent to which the providers acquired their concession or licence.

287. That annual transmission time does not include the time earmarked for news, sports events, games, advertising, teletext services and teleshopping. The proportion of European audiovisual works includes audiovisual works of in-house production and Croatian audiovisual works.

288. The mandatory proportion of European works in the programmes does not apply to television broadcasters with a local concession who are not affiliated with the national network.

C. Independent Works

289. An independent producer of audiovisual works is a legal or natural person who is registered for the production of audiovisual works and is established in the Republic of Croatia or in one of the EU Member States. He or she cannot be part of the organizational structure of a television broadcaster and neither can any television broadcaster own more than a 25% share in the capital, managerial or voter's rights of the independent producer. Furthermore, an independent producer must not realize more than one half of his annual production upon the order of one single television broadcaster.[343]

290. An independent producer is also a legal or natural person who is registered to produce audiovisual works and who has an establishment in one of the third countries if European works comprise the major part of his or her audiovisual production in the last three years. The independent producer may not be a legal or natural person whose average share in the total production or co-production costs of the productions, in which they participated in the last three years, does not exceed 10%.[344]

342. Article 4 *Ibid.*
343. Article 43 of the EMA.
344. Article 43(2,3) of the EMA.

291. Television broadcasters must reserve, to their best effort, at least 10% of the time in the annual audiovisual programme for European works produced by independent producers. Those broadcasters who cannot attain the 10% mark must progressively increase the proportion of such works every year in relation to the past year in accordance with the criteria and the method laid down in the 'Ordinance on the criteria and manner of increasing the share of the European audiovisual works of independent producers',[345] taking into account the media service broadcaster's informational, educational, cultural and entertainment responsibilities to its viewers.

292. At least half of the independent works must be produced in the previous five years. The annual transmission time does not include the time earmarked for news, sports events, prize TV games, advertising, teletext services and teleshopping. The EMA provisions for independent works do not apply to television broadcasters who have a local concession and who are not affiliated with the national network.

§4. Protection of Minors

I. General Obligations

293. With regards to the protection of minors, a general obligation is imposed on all media service providers which stipulates that it is not allowed to publish information revealing the identity of a child up to 18 years of age involved in cases of any type of violence, regardless of the child's status as witness, victim or perpetrator, or in cases of attempted suicide or committed suicide, as well as to introduce details of a child's family affairs and private life.[346]

II. Linear Audio and Audiovisual Media Services

294. According to Article 26, paragraphs 2 and 3 of the EMA, linear audio and audiovisual programmes (television and radio broadcast) which *might seriously impair* the physical, mental or moral development of minors, in particular, programmes that involve pornography or gratuitous violence are prohibited.[347]

295. Linear audio and audiovisual programmes which are *likely to impair* the physical, mental or moral development of minors are prohibited, except where it is ensured by the television or radio broadcaster, by selecting the time of the broadcast or by any technical measure, that minors in the area of transmission will not normally hear or see such broadcasts. When such programmes are broadcast in

345. Ordinance on the criteria and manner of increasing the share of the European audiovisual works of independent producers, Official Gazette [OG] No. 153/2009, 84/2011, 94/2013 and 136/2013.
346. Article 12(3) of the EMA.
347. Article 26(2) of the EMA.

unencoded form, the broadcaster must ensure that they are preceded by an acoustic warning or are identified by the presence of visual symbols throughout their duration.[348] The time of broadcast, as well as the visual symbols to be used in order to identify programmes, which are likely to impair the physical, mental or moral development of minors, are prescribed by the EMC in the 'OPM'.[349]

296. According to Article 2 of the OPM programmes that are *likely to impair* the physical, mental or moral development of minors include all types of programmes with scenes depicting explicit physical and/or verbal violence, frightening scenes of deaths or wounding, sex and sexual exploitation, vulgar language and scenes, abuse of tobacco, alcohol, narcotics, gambling, betting and other scenes. Those types of programmes won't be considered harmful if they serve to illustrate in an appropriate and meaningful manner or treat the subject in educational, formational, documentary, scientific and current affairs programmes.

297. When there is information about any form of violence in which, as a witness, a minor is involved as a victim or perpetrator, or a minor has attempted or committed suicide, the minor's identity must always be protected using a misty, quantized or masked image and a modulated tone so that the minor cannot be recognized. Such information must not disclose either the details about family relationships or about private life, nor mention the name, surname or other information that could lead to an identification of the minor and threaten the minor's well-being.[350]

298. Parts of the news programmes that are likely to impair the physical, mental or moral development of minors must be announced with a warning trigger for disturbing or violent scenes.[351]

299. It is prohibited to publish pornographic content on unencrypted channels.

300. If the programmes that are likely to impair the physical, mental or moral development of minors or compromise their integrity, self-perception, self-esteem or identity are broadcast in *unencrypted form*, the media service provider must ensure that they can be identified by visual symbols throughout their entire duration. If those programmes are broadcast in *encrypted form* media service provider must ensure that they can be recognized by written warnings (*The following programme is not suitable for persons under …*) that is broadcasted just prior to the commencement of the programme. Visual symbol by which it is possible to identify the programmes is a graphical sign in the top corner of the screen.

348. Article 26(3) of the EMA.
349. Ordinance on the protection of minors in electronic media, Official Gazette [OG] No. 28/2015.
350. Article 3 of the OPM.
351. Article 4 of the OPM.

301. According to Article 9 of the OPM, graphical signs relate to different categories of programmes that are likely to impair the physical, mental or moral development of minors and times that those programmes can be broadcasted:

Category number 18 – transparent circle and red	– may not be broadcasted between 7:00 am and 11:00 pm.
Category number 15 – transparent circle and orange	– may not be broadcasted between 7:00 am and 08:00 pm.
Category number 12 – transparent circle and green	– no time restriction, but broadcaster must ensure that programmes are preceded by an audible warning that says: 'The following programme is not suitable for persons under the age of 12 years.'

302. For radio broadcasting, in unencoded form, of audio programmes that are likely to impair the physical, mental or moral development of minors or jeopardize their integrity, self-perception, self-esteem or identity, the media service provider must ensure that they can be recognized by audio symbols. The audio symbols by which it is possible to identify such programmes are an audible warning emitted immediately prior to the commencement of the programme and the read warning: 'The following programme is not suitable for persons under 12/15/18 years of age', where the above-mentioned categories and time of broadcast also apply.[352]

III. On-Demand Audiovisual Media Services

303. With regards to the protection of minors in on-demand audiovisual media services, Article 20 of the EMA stipulates that on-demand audiovisual media services which *might seriously impair* the physical, mental or moral development of minors can only be available in such a way that minors will not in normal circumstances hear or see such on-demand audiovisual media services.

304. There are no restrictions for on-demand audiovisual media services that are *likely to impair* the physical, mental or moral development of minors, but there is an obligation according to Article 14 of the OPM for on-demand audiovisual media service providers to ensure that such programmes can be identified by means of visual symbols.

305. The visual symbols that allow identification of such programmes are written signs and offers in a particular catalogue of media service providers. When designating adopted programmes, media service providers may take into account already existing signs, but such signs may not be below the standards stipulated by

352. Article 16 of the OPM.

OPA. Furthermore, media service providers are recommended to adopt film categorizations from the database of the HAVC. Media service providers are responsible for designating all programmes, especially designating the contents of their own production.[353] When first accessing the particular catalogue, the media service provider must insist on having the PIN changed.

IV. Electronic Publications

306. As mentioned above, the provisions for the protection of minors in Article 26 of the EMA are applied accordingly in electronic publications with regards to programmes that *might seriously impair or are likely to impair* the physical, mental or moral development of minors.

307. Furthermore, Article 15 of the OPM stipulates that if an electronic publication publishes content that is *likely to impair* the physical, mental or moral development of minors or jeopardize their integrity, self-perception, self-esteem or identity of minors, the provider of electronic publications must ensure that inappropriate images or content are not published on the front page and is obligated to identify such content with written warnings indicating that the content is not suitable for persons under 18 years of age.

§5. Human Dignity

308. As a general rule, in all of the audio and audiovisual media services and electronic publications it is prohibited to promote, favour the promotion of and spreading of hatred or discrimination based on race or ethnic affiliation or colour, gender, language, religion, political or other belief, national or social origin, property, trade union membership, education, social status, marital or family status, age, health condition, disability, genetic heritage, native identity, expression or sexual orientation. Prohibited as well are the promotion, favouring of promotion or spreading of anti-Semitism and xenophobia, ideas of the fascist, nationalist, communist and other totalitarian regimes.

309. Furthermore, Article 26, paragraph 1 of the EMA explicitly prohibits the dissemination of programme in radio and television broadcast that would offend *human dignity*, contain immoral and pornographic content or in any manner encourage, promote and glorify violence and crime and encourage citizens, especially children and youth, to use tobacco products, alcohol or drugs.

353. Article 10 *Ibid.*

§6. RIGHT OF REPLY AND RIGHT TO A CORRECTION OF PUBLISHED INFORMATION

310. In the Republic of Croatia, the right of reply and the right to a correction of published information are differentiated by law. Both rights are regulated by the MA as *lex generalis* for all media service providers in Croatia. Additionally, in line with obligations stipulated in Article 41, paragraph 3 of the MA,[354] the right to correction of published information in programmes of audio and audiovisual media services is regulated by the EMC Rules for the exercise of the right to correction in programmes of audio and audiovisual media service providers (RERC).[355] Those Rules contain identical provisions as the MA but are accordingly applied to audio and audiovisual media services.

311. Article 2, paragraph 3 of the EMA stipulates that the *right to correction* of broadcast information and the *right to reply* to broadcast information shall be exercised in accordance with MA.

I. Right to a Correction of Published Information

312. As stated in Article 40, paragraph 4 of the MA (Article 1, paragraph 4 of the RERC), the right to correction of published information in the media does not refer only to a correction in the narrow sense, as a correction of wrongful statements or untruthful claims. The said right also includes the disclosure of facts and circumstances by which the affected party refutes or, with the intention to refute, significantly supplements the statements in the published text.

313. In accordance with Article 40, paragraph 1 of the MA (Article 1, paragraph 1 of the RERC), everyone has the right to request, from the editor-in-chief, the uncompensated publication of a correction of published information which has violated their rights or interests. Legal persons and other organizations and bodies are also entitled to a correction if the information is in violation of their rights and interests. The purpose of the correction is to correct untruthful or incomplete information.

314. The publication of a correction may be requested within thirty days from the publication of the information. The request for a correction should be submitted to the editor-in-chief in written form. The request must contain an explanation and the signature of the submitter, as well as all necessary information on the submitter and his or her address.[356]

354. EMC must stipulate the rules for the exercise of the right to a correction in radio and television programmes, in the manner corresponding to the nature of those media, but in such a manner that the provisions pertaining to the right to a correction and response stipulated by MA are respected as much as possible.
355. Rules for the exercise of the right to correction in programmes of audio and audiovisual media service providers, Official Gazette [OG] No. 46/2010.
356. Article 40(2,3) of the MA.

315. A scientific or artistic review shall not imply the right to a correction unless it corrects an incorrect or insulting statement. A correction may not be requested if the media itself has already published a correction of the same information by the day of submission of the request for a correction. If the submitter of the request for a correction considers that the media has not published the correction in an appropriate manner, he or she may request the realization of his or her right in compliance with MA.[357]

316. If the person to whom the information refers is deceased, the children, adopted children, spouse, parents, adoptive parents, brothers and sisters of that person shall have the right to publish a correction or a response. A legal person shall have this right if the information relates to an activity of the deceased with regard to that legal person.[358]

317. Once submitted, a correction must be published without change or addition in the same or equivalent place within the programme area, and in the same or equivalent manner as the corrected information. A correction may not be disproportionately longer than the information or part thereof to which it pertains. A correction may be published in changed form only if the submitter of the request agrees.[359]

318. According to Article 2 of the RERC, in radio and television programmes, the correction shall be made in writing and it shall be broadcast by reading it out in the same programme and in the same time-slot as the information to which the correction refers was broadcast, or in the same kind of programme with the same viewer rating. Where the programme wherein this disputed information was published as a single item or the last episode in a serial, the relevant correction shall be published in the programme which is the closest in schedule and thematically the most related.

319. An audio or audiovisual media service provider must keep records of the entire published programme for at least ninety days from the date of its original publication. In case of a complaint or a dispute the relevant provider shall keep a record of the disputed content until the dispute is resolved and provide the interested party with the appropriate copy/record of the disputed content, at the expense thereof and not later than three days after receiving the interested parties' written request.[360]

320. If within eight days after publishing the disputable information, the interested party provides a notification in writing that he or she will request the publication of a correction, the editor-in-chief or the programme manager must keep a copy of the information to which the correction refers until the publishing of the requested correction, or until the end of the court proceedings conducted in relation

357. Article 40(5,6) of the MA.
358. Article 40(7) of the MA.
359. Article 41(1) of the MA.
360. Article 4 of the RERC.

to the publishing of the disputed information, or until the expiry of the legally prescribed terms for the exercise of the right to correction or judicial protection.[361]

321. In case the concession or licence of the media service provider has expired or was revoked in the meantime, the relevant audio and/or audiovisual media service provider must ensure the publication/broadcast of the correction, at its own expense and under prescribed conditions, by another audio and audiovisual media service provider in the same area where the disputed information was published.

322. Article 7 of the RERC stipulates that its provisions can only be applied for the purpose of correcting incorrect published information. According to Article 41, paragraph 4 of the MA, in electronic publications, the correction must be marked and linked to the information it pertains to.

II. Right of Reply

323. Since there are no specific EMC rules for the right of reply to published information in programmes of audio and audiovisual media service providers, the MA provisions are applied.

324. Article 56 of the MA stipulates that the concerned natural or legal person has the right to request from the editor-in-chief the publication, free of charge, of his/her reply to published information mentioning his/her name or relating to him/her directly in some other manner. The reply can be a text or a message of identical nature as the published information. By way of allegations appropriately demonstrating evidence, the reply must, in essence, deny or significantly supplement the allegations of facts and data contained in the originally published information.

III. Publication of the Reply or Correction

325. The request for correction of published information must clearly state the information and date of publication to which the correction pertains. The correction must be published in the first equivalent daily programme or electronic publication of the relevant audio and audiovisual media service provider subsequent to the receipt of the correction. No commentary or reply to a correction can be published together with the correction within the same programme or electronic publication of the relevant audio and audiovisual media service provider.[362]

326. Any commentary or reply to a correction is considered also as a correction of published information and all of the provisions pertaining to a right to correction are applied.

361. Article 5 of the RERC.
362. Article 3(3) of the RERC.

327. A reply to published information must be published without alterations or supplements, with the exception of spelling errors. Furthermore, before the publication of the reply the editor-in-chief has a right to request from the author to shorten the reply.[363]

328. Article 42, paragraph 4 stipulates that the editor-in-chief is obligated to publish a correction or replay to published information, *except in the case* that:

- the requested correction or reply does not relate to the information which the interested person invokes;
- the requested correction or reply does not contain facts or circumstances related to the statements about the information;
- the publication of the correction or reply would be contrary to the law and good practices;
- the request for the publication of the correction or replay was not signed by the submitter of the request, i.e., the competent person from a State body or legal person;
- the requested correction or reply is disproportionately longer than the information which contains statements because of which the correction or replay is requested, or part thereof to which it directly pertains, except if the correction or reply pertains to libels or insults;
- the publication of the correction or reply would invoke liability of the publisher for compensation of damage;
- the correction or reply is written in a language that is not identical to the language in which the contested information was published;
- the request for a correction or replay of information was submitted after thirty days;
- it concerns a scientific or artistic review, except for the correction or reply of incorrect facts or insults;
- another authorized person has previously submitted a correction or reply of the same content in relation to the same information;
- the request for the publication of a correction or reply has the same content as the request for a correction or reply in relation to which court proceedings are being conducted due to the rejection or inappropriate manner of its publication;
- the submitted reply is equal in terms of content to an already published reply;[364]
- the replay contains false data, claims or allegations inadequate for the demonstration of evidence.[365] If according to the opinion of the editor-in-chief, replay contains only some data or claims that are false or inappropriate for the demonstration of evidence, the editor-in-chief cannot refuse publication of replay without previously asking the author to exclude those data and claims from the replay.[366]

---

363. Article 57 of the MA.
364. Article 57(3) of the MA.
365. Article 57(4) of the MA.
366. Article 57(5) of the MA.

329. In case that the correction or reply is not published, the editor-in-chief is obligated to inform the submitter, in writing, of the reasons for not publishing the correction or replay within the deadline stipulated for the publication of the correction or reply.

IV. Court Protection

330. Both the right to correction and the right of reply are judicially protected in the Republic of Croatia. Article 46 of the MA stipulates that, if the editor-in-chief fails to publish a correction or reply within the deadline and in accordance with the law, the person that requested the publication has the right to file a lawsuit against the editor-in-chief before a municipal court in the area in which the seat or permanent residence of the publisher of the media, which published the information to which the correction or reply pertains, is located.

331. The lawsuit may be filed within a maximum of thirty days after the expiry of the deadline for the publication of the correction or reply, or from the day when the correction was published in a manner contrary to the law.

332. Court proceedings on the publication of the correction or the reply must be resolved in an emergency court procedure. The first hearing of the main trial in proceedings for the publication of a correction or reply must take place within eight days from the submission of the lawsuit before the court. The defendant is obligated to reply to the lawsuit at the main hearing at the latest. In the summons, the court shall warn the plaintiff that the lawsuit will be considered withdrawn if he fails to appear at the first hearing. The Court will also warn the defendant that a verdict may be passed even in case of his absence.[367]

333. The discussion following a lawsuit for the publication of a correction or reply is limited to the (proof of) facts related to the defendant's duty to publish the correction. The defendant will be permitted to prove the correctness of the facts from the published information as a reason for not publishing a correction if the contested information has violated the right to privacy protected in line with the law or if the contested information refers to facts covered by the amnesty, court rehabilitation or revision of the verdict. In correction or reply publication disputes, the court will reject the claim if it determines that the plaintiff's right or interest was not denied or if it determines the existence of another circumstance due to which, according to the law, there is no obligation to publish such a correction.

334. The Court is obligated to pass a verdict immediately after the conclusion of the main hearing. The court forwards a verified copy of the verdict to the parties within a maximum of three days from the day the verdict was passed. Should the court accept the claim, it passes a verdict imposing an obligation upon the defendant to publish a correction within the deadline and in the manner stipulated by the

367. Article 47 of the MA.

MA. When publishing the correction, the editor-in-chief is obligated to state that it is a statement based on the verdict and to quote the enacting clause of the verdict.

335. The court will immediately forward a verified copy of the legally valid court verdict ordering the publication of the correction or reply to the editor-in-chief of the media in which the correction is to be published.

Chapter 4. Political Broadcasting

§1. Rules on Political Independence of Broadcasters

336. The political independence of the media in the Republic of Croatia is inseparable from the general context of media independence. Above all, freedom of the media encompasses: freedom of expression; media independence; freedom of gathering, research, publication and dissemination of information in order to inform the public; pluralism and diversity of media; freedom of information flow and media openness for diverse opinions, beliefs and diversity; access to public information; respect for the protection of human personality, privacy and dignity; freedom of establishment of legal entities for performing public information, printing and dissemination activities media from the country and abroad; production and publication of radio and television programmes, as well as other electronic media; the autonomy of editors, journalists and other authors of programme content in accordance with the rules of the profession.[368]

337. Provisions emphasizing the necessity of separation of politics and media activity can be found in the CRTA.[369] The HRT, as a public service, is under special risk of falling under the influence of politics. Hence, the CRTA stipulates that in carrying out its activities, the HRT is independent of any political influence and pressure of promoters of commercial interest. The positions of the HRT chief executive and the HRT editor-in-chief are incompatible with holding a public office, with a position within the bodies of local and regional self-government units, nor with the bodies of political parties.[370] Members of the HRT Council cannot be State officials or persons exercising their duties in the bodies of political parties or bodies of local and regional self-government units.[371]

§2. Fair Representation in Election Periods

338. The conduct of the media during elections is prescribed by two important laws; The Election of Members to the Croatian Parliament Act (EMCPA)[372] at the national level, and the Local Elections Act (LEA)[373] at the local level. Croatian Television and Croatian Radio are obliged to keep track of election promotion and during the electoral campaign period, and to allow the presentation and explanation of electoral programmes to all electoral candidates.[374] Publishers of other media

---

368. Article 3 of the MA.
369. Article 1(4) of the CRTA.
370. Article 20(3) of the CRTA.
371. Article 25(5) of the CRTA.
372. The Election of Members to the Croatian Parliament Act, Official Gazette (OG) No. 116/99, 109/00, 53/03, 69/03, 167/03, 44/06, 19/07, 20/09, 145/10, 24/11, 93/11, 120/11, 19/15, 104/15.
373. The Local Elections Act, Official Gazette (OG) No. 114/12, 121/16.
374. Article 29(1) of the EMCPA.

independently decide whether and to what extent the electoral campaign will be followed. Media publishers are obliged to guarantee journalistic independence, professionalism and expertise, consistent compliance with the journalistic code and in particular the fundamental principle of freedom of expression enshrined in the provisions of the Constitution of the Republic of Croatia, the Convention on the Protection of Human Rights and Fundamental Freedoms and the Charter of Fundamental Rights of the EU.[375]

339. Election promotion participants have equal conditions for pre-election competition and for this purpose have an equal position in representation in all local media.[376] Electronic media are obliged to respect the principle of equal access to paid political advertising of election promoters and objective, impartial and balanced information on electoral advertising.[377]

§3. News and Current Affairs Programmes

340. The Act regulating the obligations of political news broadcasters is the EMA. Audio and/or audiovisual media services that endanger constitutional order and national security are not allowed.[378] Audiovisual and/or audiovisual media services are not allowed to encourage, favour or spread hate or discrimination on grounds of race or ethnicity or colour, sex, language, religion, political or other belief, national or social origin, property status, education, social status, marital or family status, age, health status, disability, genetic heritage, gender identity, expression or sexual orientation. Neither may they encourage, favour or spread anti-Semitism and xenophobia, ideas of fascist, nationalist, communist and other totalitarian regimes.[379] Disclosure of information revealing the identity of a child under the age of 18 who is involved in any form of violence, whether as a witness, victim or perpetrator is forbidden. It is also forbidden to reveal that a child has attempted or committed suicide, or to reveal details of the child's family and private life.[380]

§4. Political Advertising

341. Advertising of political parties, coalitions and independent representatives of representative bodies is not allowed, except during an election period.[381] Political parties and coalitions should not be sponsors of audiovisual or radio programmes except during an election campaign, and at the time of such election campaign, the television and/or radio broadcaster must allow all political parties to

375. Article 29(2) of the EMCPA.
376. Article 38(1) of the LEA.
377. Article 38(2) of the LEA.
378. Article 12(1) of the EMA.
379. Article 12(2) of the EMA.
380. Article 12(3) of the EMA.
381. Article 30(3) of the EMA.

promote themselves under equal conditions in accordance with the electoral regulations and instructions of the competent body supervising or conducting the elections.[382]

382. Articles 35 and 36(8) of the EMA.

Chapter 5. Advertising Rules

§1. Various Forms of Commercial Communications

342. For the purposes of the EMA, *audiovisual commercial communication* is defined as images with or without sound which are designed to promote, directly or indirectly, the goods, services or image of a natural or legal entity pursuing an economic activity. Such images accompany or are included in a programme in return for payment or for similar consideration or for self-promotional purposes. Forms of audiovisual commercial communication include, *inter alia*, television advertising, sponsorship, teleshopping and product placement.[383]

343. *Advertising* is defined as any form of announcement broadcast in return for payment or for similar consideration, or any announcement broadcast for self-promotional purposes by a public or private undertakings or natural persons in connection with commerce, business, craft or profession in order to promote the supply of goods or services, including immovable property, rights and obligations, in return for payment.[384]

344. *Surreptitious audiovisual commercial communication* is defined as the representation in words or pictures of goods, services, the name, the trademark or the activities of a producer of goods or a service provider in programmes, when such representation is intended by the media service provider to use such representation as advertising that might mislead the public as to its nature. Such representation shall, in particular, be considered as intentional if it is done in return for payment or for similar consideration.[385]

345. *Misleading advertising* is any advertising which in any way, including its presentation, deceives or is likely to deceive the persons to whom it is addressed or whom it reaches and which, by reason of its deceptive nature, is likely to affect their economic behaviour or which, for those reasons, injures or is likely to injure a competitor.[386]

346. *Comparative advertising* is any advertising which explicitly or by implication identifies a competitor or goods or services offered by a competitor.[387]

347. *Sponsorship* is defined as any contribution made by public or private undertakings or natural persons not engaged in the provision of audiovisual media services or in the production of audiovisual works, to the financing of audiovisual

383. Article 2(14) of the EMA.
384. Article 2(15) of the EMA.
385. Article 2(16) of the EMA.
386. Article 2(17) of the EMA.
387. Article 2(18) of the EMA.

media services or programmes with a view of promoting their name, their trademark, their image, their activities or their products.[388]

348. *Teleshopping* is a direct offer, broadcast to the public, with a view to the supply of goods or services, including immovable property, rights and obligations, in return for payment.[389]

349. Finally, *product placement* is defined as any form of audiovisual commercial communication consisting of the inclusion of or reference to a product, a service or the corresponding trademark so that it is featured within a programme, in return for payment or for similar consideration.[390]

§2. Restrictions on Content

I. Audiovisual Commercial Communications

350. The EMA contains a comprehensive set of rules related to audiovisual commercial communications. All audio and audiovisual media service providers are required to make any audiovisual commercial communication readily recognizable as such. It is prohibited to broadcast surreptitious audiovisual commercial communications or to use subliminal techniques.[391]

351. Furthermore, Article 16, paragraph 4 of the EMA stipulates that audiovisual commercial communications shall not:

- prejudice the respect for human dignity;
- include or promote any discrimination based on sex, racial or ethnic origin, nationality, religion or belief, disability, age or sexual orientation;
- encourage behaviour prejudicial to health or safety;
- encourage behaviour grossly prejudicial to the protection of the environment.

352. All forms of audiovisual commercial communications for cigarettes and other tobacco products are prohibited.

353. Regarding protection of minors with from inappropriate audiovisual commercial communications, Article 16, paragraph 7 stipulates that it is prohibited to aim audiovisual commercial communications for alcoholic beverages specifically at minors or to encourage immoderate consumption of such beverages. Also, audiovisual commercial communications must not:

- cause physical or moral detriment to minors;

388. Article 2(19) of the EMA.
389. Article 2(20) of the EMA.
390. Article 2(21) of the EMA.
391. Article 16 of the EMA.

- directly encourage minors to buy or hire a product or service by exploiting their inexperience or credulity;
- directly encourage minors to persuade their parents or others to purchase the goods or services being advertised;
- exploit the special trust minors place in parents, teachers or other persons;
- unreasonably show minors in dangerous situations.

354. Pursuant to Article 10 of the EMA, that enables media service providers to regulate particular issues by self-regulation and/or co-regulation, media service providers can develop codes of conducts regarding inappropriate audiovisual commercial communication, included in or accompanying children's programmes, of foods and beverages containing nutrients and substances with a nutritional or physiological effect, in particular those such as fat, trans-fatty acids, salt/sodium and sugars, excessive intakes of which in the overall diet are not recommended.

355. Additionally, the EMC OPM provides more specific protection of minors regarding audiovisual commercial communications. Pursuant to Article 5 of the OPM:

- audiovisual commercial communications must not be physically, mentally or morally harmful to minors, nor directly encourage them to buy or rent goods and services, meaning minors personally or through their parents or other persons of their trust;
- programmes aimed at minors and shown in audiovisual commercial communications relating to food and beverages of which excessive use in a general diet is not recommended shall not use public figures nor popular characters from animated and feature-length films;
- media service providers may not broadcast audiovisual commercial messages in programmes aimed at minors where such messages promote the cult of the body, gender, age or racial stereotypes and/or discrimination. Furthermore, it is prohibited to broadcast audiovisual commercial messages that promote societal discrimination because of physical appearance or that promote success based on weight loss or based on other aesthetic categories;
- advertising of alcoholic beverages must not be aimed at minors, and in particular, minors should not be shown to consume alcohol;
- minors must not be shown in an unreasonable or attractive manner in audiovisual commercial communications in health- or life-threatening situations.

II. Advertising on Radio and Television Media Services

356. Pursuant to Article 29 of the EMA, advertising and teleshopping in radio and television media services must be readily recognizable and distinguishable from editorial content. Without prejudice to the use of new advertising techniques, advertising and teleshopping must be kept quite distinct from other parts of the programme by optical, acoustic and/or spatial means. The exceptions are isolated short advertising spots and short teleshopping spots other than in transmissions of sports events. Comparative advertising is permissible only under the conditions prescribed by the Impermissible Advertising Act.[392]

357. With regards to protection of minors in radio and television advertising and teleshopping, such communications that are aimed at minors, or using minors, must avoid anything that could jeopardize their interests. Also, their particular sensitivity and susceptibility must be taken into consideration, and a moral or physical detriment to minors must not be caused.[393]

358. Advertising which depicts women and men in an abusive or humiliating way in relation to gender and sexual orientation is prohibited. Advertising of political parties, coalitions and independent members of representative bodies is prohibited, save during the time of electoral promotion in accordance with a separate Act.[394]

359. Advertising and teleshopping for weapons and ammunition, pyrotechnical means and drugs, tobacco and tobacco products are prohibited.

360. Medicinal products can be advertised in radio and television services only if advertisement complies with the conditions stipulated in the Medicines Act[395] and the Medicinal Products Act,[396] and the subordinate legislation. Teleshopping for medicines, medicinal products, and medical treatment is prohibited.

361. Advertising and teleshopping for alcohol and alcoholic beverages are generally prohibited, unless the Food Act,[397] or the subordinate legislation passed by virtue thereof, provides otherwise. If advertising and teleshopping for some type of alcohol and alcoholic beverages (like beer and wine) are allowed, the following criteria must still be fulfilled:

- it may not be aimed specifically at minors or, in particular, depict minors consuming these beverages;
- it shall not link the consumption of alcohol to enhanced physical performance or to driving;
- it shall not create the impression that the consumption of alcohol contributes towards social or sexual success;
- it shall not claim that alcohol has therapeutic qualities or that it is a stimulant, a sedative or a means of resolving personal conflicts;
- it shall not encourage immoderate consumption of alcohol or present abstinence or moderation in a negative light;

392. Impermissible Advertising Act, Official Gazette [OG] No. 43/2009.
393. Article 30(1) of the EMA.
394. Article 30(2) of the EMA.
395. Medicines Act, Official Gazette [OG] No. 76/2013, 90/2014.
396. Medicinal Products Act, Official Gazette [OG] No. 76/2013.
397. Food Act, Official Gazette [OG] No. 81/2013, 14/2014, 30/2015.

– it shall not place emphasis on high alcoholic content as being a positive quality of the beverages.

§3. Time and Frequency Restrictions

I. Sponsorship

A. *Restrictions Regarding Sponsorship*

362. Article 17 of the EMA stipulates that in the case of sponsorship of audio and audiovisual media services or programmes their content, or in the case of television broadcasting their scheduling, may not be in any circumstances influenced in such a way as to affect the responsibility and editorial independence of the media service provider.

363. Audio and audiovisual media services and programmes that are sponsored may not directly encourage the purchase or rental of goods or services, in particular by making special promotional references to those goods or services.

364. Viewers must be clearly informed of the existence of a sponsorship agreement. Sponsored programmes must be clearly identified as such by the name, logo or any other symbol of the sponsor such as, for example, a reference to its products or services or a distinctive sign thereof in an appropriate way for these programmes at the beginning, during and at the end of the programmes.

B. *Prohibited Sponsorship*

365. Audio and audiovisual media services or programmes may not be sponsored by a company whose principal activity is the manufacturing or sale of cigarettes or other tobacco products. If audio or audiovisual media services or programmes are sponsored by a company whose activities include the manufacture or sale of medicinal products and medical treatments, the promotion of the name or the image of this company is allowed, but a promotion of specific medicinal products or medical treatments available only on prescription is prohibited.

366. News and current affairs programmes may not be sponsored. Also, showing a logo during children's programmes and religious programmes is prohibited.

367. According to Article 35 of the EMA, political parties and coalitions may not be the sponsors of audiovisual or radio programmes except during the time of electoral promotion in compliance with a special Act.

II. Product Placement

A. General Prohibition of Product Placement

368. Article 18 of the EMA *prohibits product placement* except in the cases defined by the EMA.

369. Product placement is *permitted* in cinematographic works, films and series made for audiovisual media services, sports programmes and light entertainment programmes, with the exception of children's programmes

370. Product placement is also *permitted in cases where there is no payment* to the media services provider, but certain goods or services are provided free of charge, such as production props and prizes, with a view to their inclusion in an audiovisual programme. In those cases, it is assumed that the product placement exists if the goods or services involved in the audiovisual programme are of significant value. The EMC must determine by an Ordinance the manner of determining the significant value of the goods and services placed taking into account that the significant value is assessed in relation to the budget of the production or the costs paid for the product placement of the product or service in this programme.

371. In any case, audiovisual programmes may not contain product placement of tobacco products or cigarettes or product placement of a company whose principal activity is the manufacture or sale of cigarettes and other tobacco products, or specific medicinal products or medical treatments available only on prescription.

B. Product Placement Requirements

372. Audiovisual programmes that contain product placement *must meet the following requirements*:

- their content and, in the case of television broadcasting, their scheduling may in no circumstances be influenced in such a way as to affect the responsibility and editorial independence of the media service provider;
- they may not directly encourage the purchase or rental of goods or services, in particular by making special promotional references to those goods or services;
- they may not give undue prominence to the product in question;
- viewers must be clearly informed of the existence of product placement;
- they must be appropriately identified at the start and the end of the audiovisual programme and when an audiovisual programme resumes after an advertising break, in order to avoid any confusion on the part of the viewer. The exception is when the audiovisual programme containing product placement has neither been produced nor commissioned by the media service provider itself or a company affiliated with the media service provider.

Chapter 6. Right to Information

§1. Access to Major Events

373. Pursuant to Article 46 of the EMA, television broadcasters may not, on an exclusive basis, broadcast events which are regarded as being of major importance for society in such a way as to deprive a substantial proportion of the public in the Republic of Croatia of the possibility of following such events by live coverage or deferred coverage on free television.

374. The EMC must draw up a list of designated events, national or non-national, which it considers to be of major importance for society and it must also determine whether these events should be available by whole or partial live coverage, or where necessary or appropriate for objective reasons in the public interest, whole or partial deferred coverage. Furthermore, the EMC must immediately notify the European Commission of that list and other measures taken, so that the Commission may verify whether such measures are compatible with Union law and communicates them to the other Member States of the EU.

375. The list of major events that was drafted by EMC in 2008[398] in Article 4. comprises:

- Summer and Winter Olympic Games;
- finals of World and European football championship, all games that are played by Croatian national team and an opening game of those championships;
- all games of senior Croatian national football team, at home and away;
- finals of Croatian football Cup;
- finals and semi-finals of Champions League and UEFA Cup if Croatian teams are taking part;
- finals of Grand Slam tournaments (Wimbledon, Roland Garros, US Open, Australian Open) if Croatian players are taking part;
- finals of ATP and WTA tournaments in Croatia;
- final competitions of World and European championship in athletics if Croatian athletes are taking part;
- finals of World and European handball, basketball, water polo and swimming championships if Croatian national teams or athletes are taking part;
- finals of handball Champions League if Croatian team is taking part;
- ski championships in Croatia;
- opening ceremonies of events of national importance: *Split summer festival*, *Dubrovnik summer festival*, *Varaždin baroque evenings*, *Osor musical evenings*.

376. It is *contrary* to the EMA for an event of major importance, which is broadcast on the basis of exclusive rights by a television broadcaster, to be *viewable by*

398. List of Major Events of the EMC, available at: https://www.e-mediji.hr/files/podzakonski/2009_4 1.pdf (16 Aug. 2016).

less than 60% of the population of the Republic of Croatia or if additional payments are required (pay TV) to view that programme, other than the fees laid down in the CRTA (licence fee).

§2. Short News Reporting

377. Article 45, paragraph 6 of the EMA defines *short news* as an announcement which lasts one and a half minute at most, and which is presented as part of a general news programme.

378. For the purpose of short news reports, any television or radio broadcaster established in the EU has access under the equal conditions to events of high interest to the public which are transmitted on an exclusive basis by a television or radio broadcaster under the jurisdiction of the Republic of Croatia.

379. If a television or radio broadcaster established in the Republic of Croatia has acquired exclusive rights to the event of high interest to the public, another television or radio broadcaster established in the Republic of Croatia may seek access to the mentioned event from that television or radio broadcaster. All television or radio broadcasters have the right to access events of high interest to the public under *equal conditions.*

380. The EMC must ensure[399] that access to events of high interest to the public is guaranteed by allowing other television or radio broadcaster to freely choose short extracts from the live transmitting television or radio broadcaster's signal with at least the identification of their source unless it is impossible to do so for reasons of practicality.

381. Before and/or instead of accessing the live transmitting signal, other television or radio broadcasters may also gain physical access to events for purposes of recording short extracts or use the taped material of other television or radio broadcaster which has exclusive rights for the transmitting of the event of high interest to the public.[400]

382. Short extracts may be used solely for *general news programmes* and may be used in on-demand audiovisual media services only if the same programme is offered on a deferred basis by the same media service provider.

399. According to Article 45, paragraph 3 of the EMA, the way of ensuring the access to the transmitting signal should be stipulated by the EMC Ordinance, upon the previous opinion of the Croatian Regulatory Authority for Network Industries. Ordinance is not yet enacted.

400. Article 45 paragraph 4 of the EMA.

383. Television or radio broadcasters who broadcast the event of high interest to the public have the right to ask from another television or radio broadcaster for compensation of the actual costs incurred in the fulfilment of its obligation for short news reporting. The foreseen compensation may not exceed the additional costs directly incurred by allowing access.

384. Television or radio broadcasters, who used the right to short news reports shall enable television or radio broadcasters who could not tape the event a single use of the tape and have the right to ask compensation for this use, proportional to its share in the actual costs, as well as the mentioning of taping broadcaster's name or the name of the company in the announcement.

385. The right to short news reports must be executed in a manner which does not interrupt the course of events. If an event of high interest to the public is composed of several organizationally self-contained elements, each self-contained element is considered to be an event of high interest to the public. If an event of high interest to the public takes place over two or more days, the television or radio broadcaster has the right to produce one short news report for each day.

Chapter 7. Access to Networks

§1. Must-Carry Rules

386. Must-carry rules are prescribed by the ECA. On the basis of a decision adopted by the authority competent for electronic media on must-carry obligations concerning one or more radio and/or television programmes in the Republic of Croatia at the national, regional or other levels, Croatian Regulatory Authority for Network Industries (HAKOM) shall adopt a decision designating operators of public communications networks which are obliged to carry such programmes.[401]

387. The must-carry obligations may be imposed in compliance with the principles of proportionality and transparency, only on those operators of public communications networks which are used by a significant number of end-users as their main means of receiving radio and television programmes, and only if there is a public interest thereof.[402] The fee for carrying these programmes shall be determined in accordance with their obligations and with the principles of proportionality, transparency and non-discrimination.[403] HAKOM shall regularly verify the implementation of the must-carry obligations and every operator of the public communications network, that has been imposed the must-carry obligations, shall be entitled to request HAKOM to re-examine these obligations after the expiry of the period of four years following the adoption of the decision.[404]

§2. Other Access Obligations for Networks

388. Additional obligations exist for Significant Market Powers. An operator shall be deemed to have significant market power if, either individually or jointly with other operators, it enjoys a position equivalent to dominance, that is to say, a position of economic strength affording it the power to behave to an appreciable extent independently of competitors, users and consumers.[405]

389. HAKOM may impose obligations on operators with the significant market power to meet reasonable requirements for access to and use of specific network elements and the associated infrastructure and associated facilities.[406] This obligation may be imposed on the operators by HAKOM in particular where it considers that denial of access, or other unreasonable terms and conditions, or restrictions having a similar effect, would hinder the emergence of a sustainable competitive market at the retail level, or would not be in the end-users' interest.[407]

---

401. Article 97(1) of the ECA.
402. Article 97(2) of the ECA.
403. Article 97(3) of the ECA.
404. Article 97(4) of the ECA.
405. Article 55(1) of the ECA.
406. Article 61(1) of the ECA.
407. Article 61(2) of the ECA.

390. Operators of public communications networks shall have the right and, when requested by other operators of public communications networks, the obligation to negotiate interconnection with each other for the purpose of providing publicly available electronic communications services, in order to ensure provision and interoperability of services.[408] Operators with significant market power must offer access and interconnection to other operators in accordance with terms and conditions arising from regulatory obligations imposed by HAKOM.[409]

408. Article 61(3) of the ECA.
409. Article 61(4) of the ECA.

Chapter 8. Standards and Interoperability

391. Interconnection can be defined as special access between operators of public communications networks establishing physical and logical linking of communications networks used by the same or several different operators in order to allow the users of one operator to communicate with users of the same or of other operators or to access services provided by other operators where services may be provided by interconnected parties or other parties who have access to the network.[410]

392. Operators may negotiate or conclude contracts about technical and commercial solutions for access and/or interconnection at the national and international level.[411] An operator requesting or granting access and/or interconnection shall not be obliged to notify HAKOM in advance unless it provides electronic communications networks and services in the Republic of Croatia.[412] Operators of public communications networks shall have a right and, when requested by other operators of public communications networks, an obligation to negotiate interconnection with each other for the purpose of providing publicly available electronic communications services, in order to ensure provision and interoperability of services.[413] Operators with significant market power must offer access and interconnection to other operators in accordance with terms and conditions arising from regulatory obligations imposed by HAKOM.[414] Operators which acquired information from another operator before, during or after the process of negotiating access or interconnection may use that information solely for the purpose for which it was supplied while respecting the confidentiality of information. The received information shall not be passed on to any other party, in particular, other departments, subsidiaries or partners, for whom such information could provide a competitive advantage.[415] In disputes concerning access and interconnection, HAKOM shall, ex officio or upon request of any of the parties, adopt a decision imposing obligations on operators that control access to its end-users in order to ensure end to end connectivity.[416] This, in particular, includes the obligation to interconnect networks where this is not already the case and the imposition of technical or operational conditions to ensure normal operation of the network.[417] Obligations and terms and conditions imposed shall be objective, transparent, proportionate and non-discriminatory.[418]

---

410. Article 2(32) of the ECA.
411. Article 66(1) of the ECA.
412. Article 66(2) of the ECA.
413. Article 66(3) of the ECA.
414. Article 66(4) of the ECA.
415. Article 66(5) of the ECA.
416. Article 66(6) of the ECA.
417. *Ibid.*
418. Article 66(7) of the ECA.

Part IV. Cross-ownership Regulation

393. The regulation of allowed ownership shares in classic and electronic media is regulated at several levels in the legal order of Croatia. First of all, the general rule relevant to the above issues is the Competition Protection Act (COPA).[419] Furthermore, specific issues are to some extent resolved in the MA and the EMA.

394. It is important to note that the MA and EMA in the relevant sections indicate the need for implementing the provisions of the COPA. The MA provides that the publishers, legal persons engaged in the distribution of media, as well as other legal entities engaged in activities related to public information, are subject to the provisions of the COPA. Similarly, the EMA stipulates that the providers of media services are subject to competition regulations. Accordingly, we will, first, show the general regulation of ownership in the Republic of Croatia and, only after that, we will concentrate on media and electronic media.

395. The most important provisions of the COPA in the context of regulation of media ownership are the provisions on concentration. Concentration results from a change of control of an undertaking on a permanent basis which is accomplished with the merging or combining of two or more independent undertakings or parts of such undertakings, the acquisition of direct or indirect control or decisive influence of one or more undertakings over another or more other undertakings or in part, or parts of other companies:

- with the acquisition of the majority of shares or units; or
- with the acquisition of voting rights;
- or otherwise in accordance with the provisions of the COPA.[420]

396. Gaining control is achieved by transferring the rights, contracts or other means by which one or more undertakings, either individually or jointly, taking into account all legal and factual circumstances, gains the possibility of exercising decisive influence over one or more undertakings on a lasting basis.[421]

397. Concentration that can significantly distort competition is forbidden, especially if such distortion of competition is a result of the strengthening of an existing

419. Competition Protection Act, Official Gazette [OG] No. 79/09, 80/13.
420. Article 15 of the COPA.
421. *Ibid.*

dominant position, or the creation of a new dominant position by the merging parties.[422] The existence of concentration in any market, including in the media market, is established by the Agency for Protection of Competition (APC).

398. Potential participants in the concentration are required to report to the APC any intention of concentration if they cumulatively meet the following conditions: a total annual consolidated turnover of all parties to the concentration realized by the sale of goods and/or services on the world market is at least HRK 1 billion according to financial statements for the financial year preceding the concentration; if at least one party to the concentration has a seat and/or a branch in the Republic of Croatia; and the total turnover of each of at least two parties to the concentration, in the Republic of Croatia, according to the financial statements, amounts to at least HRK 100 million in the financial year preceding the concentration.[423]

399. During the assessment of the concentration, the APC will determine its effects on competition, and possible obstacles to market access, particularly in cases where the concentration creates a new or strengthens a dominant position of the merging parties. In assessing the effects of a merger APC determines in particular:

- structure of the relevant market, existing and possible future competitors in the relevant market on Croatian territory or outside, structure and selection of supply and demand in the market and its trends, cost, risks, economic, legal and other barriers to entry or exit from the market;
- position, market shares and economic and financial power in the relevant market, the level of competitiveness of the merging parties, possible changes in the operations of the merging parties and alternative sources of supply for customers that arise as a result of the concentration;
- the effects of concentration to other businesses or to consumers, such as shorter routes of distribution, lowered costs of distribution, specialization in production, technological innovation, lowered product and/or service prices, as well as other benefits that directly result from the merger.[424]

400. The APC decides ex officio with a special decision about the necessary measures for monitoring businesses or structural measures necessary to restore competition in the relevant market, and sets deadlines for their execution in cases where: the concentration is carried out contrary to the decision of the APC declaring it forbidden or where the concentration has been implemented without the submission of the mandatory notification of concentration. Some of the measures that can be applied by the APC in this situation are: to order the sale or transfer of acquired shares or holdings; to prohibit or restrict the exercise of voting rights attached to the

422. Article 16 of the COPA.
423. Article 17 of the COPA.
424. Article 2 of the COPA.

shares in participating companies in the concentration; and to order the termination of a joint venture or other forms of acquisition of control which led to the unauthorized transaction.[425]

401. Further, it is necessary to demonstrate the specificity of concentration and regulation of ownership in the media and the electronic media. The MA has a few provisions related to concentration. In addition to the provisions which indicate the application of the COPA, there are a few that establish specific rules for traditional media. Thus, the publishers participating in concentration are obliged to submit the notification of concentration in a form and manner established by the COPA, and the application must be submitted to the APC.[426]

402. Rules about illicit concentration are prescribed in Article 36. It is prescribed that any concentration of undertakings in the market of daily or weekly newspapers is inadmissible if the market share of the participating undertakings after the concentration would be over 40% of the daily or weekly newspaper market in Croatia. A publisher with an illicit concentration cannot acquire shares in information daily or weekly newspapers.[427]

403. The EMA, unlike the MA, has significantly more detailed provisions for the regulation of the concentration. Thus, the media service providers are required by 31 January of each calendar year to provide information on the legal person and headquarters, and the names and whereabouts of all legal and natural persons who directly or indirectly became holders of shares or equity in the media service provider, with data on the percentage of shares or units, to the EMC. To the media service providers who fail to perform this obligation, the EMC will send a written warning on the grounds of possible sanctions if they fail to comply. The media service provider is obliged to publish the aforementioned data in the Official Gazette. It is prohibited to disguise the ownership structure of the media service provider and ownership of the acquirer of shares or units in a media service provider in any legal transaction. Legal transactions that conceal the ownership structure of the media service provider and ownership of the acquirer of shares or units in a media service provider are invalid.[428] A concentration is considered impermissible in the sense of EMA if:

- A television and/or radio broadcaster has a concession at the State level and an equity interest in another publisher, which has the same kind of concessions or concession on the regional, county, municipal or city level, of more than 25%, and vice versa.
- A television and/or radio broadcaster has a concession at the State level and an equity interest in a publisher of a daily newspaper with a print run of more than 3,000 copies, of more than 10%, and vice versa.

425. Article 24 of the COPA.
426. Article 36 of the MA.
427. Article 36 of the MA.
428. Article 53 of the EMA.

- A television and/or radio broadcaster has a concession at the State level and an equity interest in a legal entity conducting news activities with a share of more than 10%, and vice versa.
- A television and/or radio broadcaster which has a concession at the State level and at the same time publishes a daily newspaper which is printed in a circulation of more than 3,000 copies.
- A television and/or radio broadcaster which has a concession on the local or regional level and an equity interest in another publisher of such regional or local level of coverage in the same area with more than 30%.
- A television and/or radio broadcaster which has a concession on a regional or local level and at the same time, in the same or adjacent area, publishes daily newspapers of local importance.
- A media service provider under Article 79 of the EMA which simultaneously publishes a daily newspaper printed in a circulation of more than 3,000 copies.
- A media service provider under Article 79 of the EMA which has an equity interest in the publisher of the daily newspaper which is circulated in more than 3,000 copies, with a share of more than 10%, and vice versa.[429]

404. The EMC will not give concessions to the most favourable bidder selected in the procedure for granting concessions if it is found that by giving concessions the result would be an impermissible concentration. Each applicant shall also offer to submit a statement that by gaining the concession an impermissible concentration would not occur.[430]

405. Any change in the ownership structure of a television and/or radio broadcaster and media service provider must be applied in writing to the EMC. If the EMC establishes that the resulting changes in the ownership structure represent an impermissible concentration in the media sector, it shall order the television and/or radio broadcaster and media service provider to adjust its ownership structure in a way that is not inconsistent with the provisions of the EMA, in a specified timeframe. If the television and/or radio broadcaster does not comply with the EMC's order, the provisions on termination of the concession will be applied, and the EMC will issue a decision on revocation of the concession. If the media service provider fails to comply with the EMC's order, the provisions on termination of permission for satellite, Internet, cable and other forms of transmission of audiovisual and/or radio programme will apply.[431] A domestic legal person whose founders are foreign legal persons registered in countries where according to the regulations of these countries it is not permitted or not possible to determine the origin of the initial capital, cannot participate in the concession granting procedure.

406. A publisher can only perform television media service or radio media services. This limit does not apply if the publisher obtains the EMC's approval, and in the case where the television and radio media services are not performed in the same

429. Article 54 of the EMA.
430. Article 56 of the EMA.
431. Article 57 of the EMA.

area.[432] A legal person whose activities consist of collecting and transmitting advertisements, as well as a natural or legal person and a group of related parties, which, in the capital or assets of this type, has more than 10% ownership interest or more than 10% of control or voting rights cannot be a television and/or radio broadcaster and/or the broadcasters founder, nor may it have owned shares in the capital of television and/or radio broadcasters. If the EMC establishes an illicit change in ownership structure, it shall order the television and/or radio broadcaster to adjust its ownership structure in a way that is not inconsistent with the EMA, in a certain timeframe. If the television and/or radio broadcaster does not comply with the EMC's order, the provisions of the EMA on the termination of the concession are applied, and the EMC issues a decision on revocation of the concession.[433] The operator carrying out the transmission of audiovisual and/or radio programmes cannot be a television and/or radio broadcaster or a media service provider over satellite, Internet, cable and other forms of transmission of audiovisual and/or radio programmes. The provisions on the ownership and concentration shall also apply to foreign legal and natural persons, regardless of in which country they have their head office or permanent residence.[434]

407. The Fund for the Promotion of Pluralism and Diversity of Electronic Media (the Fund) affects the concentration of ownership and pluralism in the media in Croatia on the specific and concrete way. This is a fund of the Electronic Media Agency. The Fund is financed through the provisions of the EMA and the CRTA.

408. The Fund will encourage the production and publication of audiovisual and radio programmes and content of the television and/or radio broadcaster at a local and regional level, non-profit television and/or radio broadcasters, non-profit providers of media services, non-profit providers of electronic publications, non-profit producers of audiovisual and/or radio programmes, which are of public interest and are especially important for:

- the exercise of the right of citizens to public information;
- the encouragement of cultural diversity and fostering heritage;
- the development of education;
- the development of science;
- the development of art;
- fostering creativity in the dialects of the Croatian language;
- the encouragement of specific cultural projects and events;
- national minorities in Croatia;
- the encouragement of awareness development on gender equality and other highest values of the constitutional order;
- raising awareness about equality of gender identity and sexual orientation;
- the encouragement of high-quality programmes for children and young people to promote their well-being;

432. Article 59 of the EMA.
433. Article 60 of the EMA.
434. Article 62 of the EMA.

- raising public awareness of the capabilities and contributions of persons with disabilities, and to promote and respect their rights and dignity, including the fight against stereotypes, prejudices and harmful practices relating to people with disabilities;
- the historically accurate presentation of the War of Independence;
- the development and promotion of media literacy programmes;
- environmental protection;
- the promotion of health and encouragement of health culture.[435]

409. The Fund will be used in order to employ highly skilled workers for the television and/or radio broadcasters at the local and regional level, non-profit television and/or radio broadcasters, non-profit providers of media services, non-profit providers of electronic publications and non-profit producers of audiovisual and/or radio programmes. The criteria for the allocation of the Fund are: the value of audiovisual and/or radio programme or the content of electronic publications for the achievement of the objectives of the EMA; the quality and innovativeness of the proposed audiovisual and/or radio programme or the content of electronic publications; interest in general or local or regional cultural development; and the availability of programmes and facilities for people with disabilities.

410. The assets of the Fund cannot be awarded to the television and/or radio broadcasters, non-profit providers of media services and non-profit providers of electronic publications which EMC reprimanded in the previous twelve months and/or those who committed misdemeanours in the previous twelve months on the basis of a final court decision for violation of EMA provisions, as well as to those who do not have media status.

411. Based on these criteria, the EMC, with the prior opinion of the relevant ministry, issues a general Act which prescribes the method and procedure of implementation of public tenders for co-financing of audiovisual and radio programme content and electronic publications from the Fund, the Fund's resource allocation ratios between different types of user agents, the monitoring of the use of funds and achievement of programmes and facilities for which they are assigned. A list of beneficiaries of the funds, programmes and content for which the funds are assigned and a report on their achievement will be published on the website of the EMC. The decision on allotment of resources is issued by the EMC.

412. The EMC is authorized to engage professionals to assist in the evaluation of applications to tender for the allocation of the Fund's resources. These professionals can be from the ranks of public employees who are media professionals and experts in audiovisual activities, prominent intellectuals, recognized artists and other public figures who have made significant efforts for the development of civil society, the defence of human rights and freedoms, the promotion of culture, science and art, as well as the protection of freedom of media and expression. The scope and methods of work of these professionals are prescribed by the EMC.[436]

435. Article 64(1) of the EMA.

Part V. Supervision: Media Regulator

Chapter 1. Organization

413. The Electronic Media Agency is in charge of regulating the provision of media services in the Republic of Croatia. The Electronic Media Agency is a legally registered independent legal entity, whose headquarters are in Zagreb. It adopts a statute approved by *Sabor*. The bodies of the Electronic Media Agency are the director and the EMC.

414. The director represents and manages the Electronic Media Agency and is responsible for the operation of professional services. The President of the Council is the Agency's director. In directing the Agency, the director organizes and manages its work and operations.

415. The salary of the director and members of the Council is determined by *Sabor* at the proposal of the Croatian government. The funds of the Electronic Media Agency, including funds for the salary of the members of the Council, shall be provided in accordance with the Agency's annual financial plan from the amount of 0.5% of the total annual gross revenue in the previous year by media service providers carrying out activities to provide audio and/or audiovisual media services in accordance with Article 19 of the EMA, the activities of providing television and/or radio media services in accordance with Articles 22 and 79 of the EMA and the activities and the provision of services of electronic publications in accordance with Article 80 of the EMA. Unused funds can be used for the Agency's long-term projects. The director shall submit an annual report to *Sabor*, which is an integral part of the report on the work of the Council.[437]

416. The Council has seven members, one of whom is the President of the Council. The president and other members of the Council are appointed and dismissed by *Sabor* at the proposal of the Croatian government. In the process of nominating members of the Council, the Croatian government publishes a public call for nomination. The president and members of the Council are appointed for a period of five

436. Article 64 of the EMA.
437. Article 67 of the EMA.

years and may be reappointed. The Deputy Chairman of the Council, on the proposal of the President of the Council, is elected by the Council by a majority vote.[438]

417. Members of the Council can only be Croatian citizens who have professional knowledge, skills and experience in radio or television, or in publishing, cultural or similar activities. Council members should be public figures who are publicly recognized for their respect for democratic principles and the rule of law, development and promotion of the highest values of Croatian constitutional system, the development of civil society, the defence of human rights and freedoms, as well as for the protection of freedom of expression. A Council member may not be a public official, an official in the executive or judicial authority or an official of a political party.[439]

418. Council members must not be owners, stakeholders or shareholders, board members, supervisory board or members of the administrative council and other relevant governing bodies, directors, nor managers or other leaders of the legal persons to which the provisions of the EMA apply. Council members cannot be employees, contractually bound, nor in any other relation to any legal person or service that is related to audio and audiovisual media services or network operators, nor persons engaged in businesses that may cause a conflict of interest.

419. Members of the Council shall not receive gifts, accept services or enter into relationships that are bringing them into a conflict of interest in relation to the tasks prescribed in the EMA.[440]

420. *Sabor* may dismiss the president or a member of the Council before the end of the term on the proposal of the Croatian government, in case:

- he or she submits a request for dismissal;
- it is determined that the member of the Council presented false data about him or herself or failed to present information on circumstances relevant to the determination of the proposal;
- he or she seriously violates the duties established by the Agency's Statute;
- he or she is unable to properly perform his or her duties for more than six months continuously;
- he or she is permanently unable to perform these duties;
- he or she is convicted of a crime;
- he or she fails to meet the objectives and tasks set forth in the Agency's annual work programme.[441]

---

438. Article 68(1, 2, 3, 4) of the EMA.
439. Article 68(5,6,7) of the EMA.
440. Article 68(8,9,10) of the EMA.
441. Article 68 para. 11, EMA.

421. Before the decision on dismissal, the President or the member of the Council must be allowed to express their opinion on the reasons for dismissal.[442] The president, vice president and member of the Council may not be appointed to the board, supervisory board or administrative council in legal entities which are subject to provisions of the EMA for a period of one year from their date of dismissal.[443]

442. Article 68 para. 12, EMA.
443. Article 68 paras 13, 14, EMA.

Chapter 2. Tasks

422. The Electronic Media Council:

- carries out the procedure to grant concessions in accordance with the EMA and the Concessions Act;
- enters into concession contracts with the highest bidder in accordance with the EMA;
- makes decisions to revoke concessions and permits in the cases provided for by the EMA;
- takes appropriate measures to temporarily restrict the freedom of transmission of audiovisual services from other countries in accordance with Article 77 of the EMA;
- carries out the procedure to grant permission for the provision of audio and/or audiovisual media services on-demand and for satellite, Internet, cable and other forms of transmission of audiovisual and/or radio programme;
- issues warnings in the event of non-compliance with the provisions of the EMA as well as the by-laws and/or submits accusatory motions in accordance with the EMA and the MDA;
- adopts its Rules of Procedure;
- keeps registers of the media service providers;
- gives his or her approval for the provision of media services, television and radio media services in case the TV and radio media service providers do not broadcast in the same area;
- carries out EMA provisions relating to the protection of pluralism and diversity of electronic media;
- provides control over the implementation of the programme, the principles and the obligations stipulated by the EMA and special laws;
- provides control of audiovisual and radio programmes that are broadcast via satellite, Internet, cable and other permitted forms of transmission;
- provides control of the designated use of the Fund;
- carries out the process of determining non-compliance or violations of the provisions of the EMA;
- considers citizens' complaints about the conduct of the media service provider in implementing the EMA, and takes measures in accordance with the EMA;
- issues recommendations related to the implementation of the EMA;
- encourages self-regulation and co-regulation in order to better implement the EMA;
- cooperates with the regulatory authorities of other countries and/or the European Commission in the exchange of information in order to implement the EMA;
- submits reports to *Sabor* and other competent bodies, in accordance with the EMA and other regulations;
- submits reports to the Commission, in accordance with the EMA and other regulations;
- works on the improvement of media literacy;
- organizes public consultations and conferences and conducts research related to specific issues in the field of electronic media;

– adopts the EMA's annual work programme; and
– carries out other duties prescribed by the EMA and the Agency Statute.[444]

423. The EMC published a notice of intent to award concessions for the provision of television and radio on a technical basis determined by HAKOM in accordance with the regulations on electronic communications. The notice shall be published for free radio frequencies or more radio frequencies that make up a separate concession or, in the case of digital radio and television, for available transmission capacity of a separate radio or television programme channel within the multiplex.[445]

424. The criteria for granting television and radio concessions are:

– programme requirements pursuant to the EMA, and especially the amount of own production, European audiovisual works and works by independent producers;
– the time of broadcast;
– the quality and diversity of audiovisual and/or radio programmes;
– special technical, financial (funding and financial guarantees) and personnel conditions;
– compliance with the provisions of the EMA and regulations governing tax and other obligations of legal entities to the State budget and the budget of local and regional governments and legal persons in their ownership.[446]

425. Offers based on the notification shall contain evidence that the conditions prescribed by the notification are met, a programme basis in accordance with the EMA, information on the ownership structure of the legal person submitting the tender, personal information about the company, or the name and place of residence of persons who directly or indirectly, or through other legal persons, have stocks or shares in that legal person, as well as data on the percentage of the shares or units. The offer must contain information on the financial capacity of bidders to provide television and/or radio broadcasting services.[447]

426. Before making a decision on granting a concession, the EMC is authorized to exchange information on the best bidder with the regulatory authorities of other EU Member States, if businesses will also be providing television and radio to the other Member States of the EU. The decision on granting a concession is made by the EMC after this tendering procedure and the procedure of determining the conditions for grant of the concession.[448]

427. The decision on granting of the concession shall contain:

444. Article 69 of the EMA.
445. Article 71(1,2) of the EMA.
446. Article 71(4) of the EMA.
447. Article 71(5) of the EMA.
448. Article 71(6,7) of the EMA.

- the name of the concession provider;
- the number and the date of the decision;
- the name of the selected best bidder;
- the basic rights and obligations of the concession provider and concessionaire;
- the obligation of the concessionaire to begin work on all assigned radio frequencies in half the time he was given the concession for at the latest;
- the nature and subject of the concession;
- the nature, extent and area for which the concession is to be used;
- the period for which the concession is granted;
- certain special conditions with which the concessionaire must comply for the duration of the concession;
- the amount of the concession fee or the basis in order to determine the amount of the concession fee;
- the timeframe within which the selected preferred bidder shall be obliged to enter into a concession contract with the concession provider, and the consequences of non-compliance with the deadline for the signing of the concession agreement;
- explanation of the reasons for the selection of the winning bidder;
- instructions on legal remedy, since this is an obligatory part of every administrative act in Croatian law, and the instructions must contain the deadline for filing the appeal or lawsuit and the administrative body or court competent for the appeal or lawsuit;
- the signature and the seal of the concession provider.[449]

428. The right to broadcast television and/or radio media services is based on a decision on granting the concession and the signing of the concession agreement. On the basis of the decision on granting the concession, the EMC signs the concession contract with the highest bidder. The concession contract, in addition to the essential conditions for the realization of the concession, must include the programme basis and other conditions of the bid for the concession. If the successful tenderer fails to sign a concession agreement that was made in writing in accordance with both the tender documents, the data from the notice of intent to grant the concession, the selected bid and the decision on granting a concession in the set deadline, the EMC shall annul the concession grant, in which case the bidder would not be entitled to compensation. It is not allowed to transfer a television and/or radio services concession.[450]

429. The area of the concession can be the national, regional, county, city, municipal or different level, as determined by a special regulation. The area of the concession at the State level must cover at least 60% of the Croatian population and, at the regional level, at least 70% of the population of the region. The concession is given for a period no longer than fifteen nor less than eight years. The concession fee is considered to be income of the State budget. The amount and method of payment of the concession fee is prescribed by the EMC, as well as the amount and method of payment for tender documents and the bid submitted under the notice of

449. Article 71(8) of the EMA.
450. Article 74 of the EMA.

intent to award a concession. Concessions for the provision of television and/or radio are entered in the register administered by the EMC and the register of concessions held at the Ministry of Finance. The content and management of the register is prescribed by the EMC Regulations.[451]

451. Article 75 of the EMA.

Chapter 3. Sanctioning Powers

430. The EMC will issue a decision on the temporary or permanent revocation of the concession or permission for the media service providers if it finds:

- that the concession is based on false information relevant to the selection of the winning bidder;
- the television and/or radio broadcaster failed to commence the concession in the period specified in the concession agreement or has not respected the technical conditions of the concession agreement for more than a month since the beginning of the concession, or suspended the operation of the concession for more than forty-eight hours;
- the media service provider, even after the third warning of the Council, which it imposed in the previous twelve months, violates the provisions of the EMA and regulations adopted pursuant to the EMA, or the concession agreement;
- if the media service provider, even after receiving a warning from the EMC does not comply with at least 90% of the programme base;
- if the media service provider, even after receiving a warning from the EMC does not respect the broadcasting time;
- if the media service provider stopped a second media service provider from exercising its right to short information contrary to the EMC order;
- if the media service provider has not paid the fee for the concession on more than two consecutive terms or generally irregularly pays the compensation for concession;
- the media service provider did not, even after receipt of a reminder from the EMC, submit the data on a change of information;
- the media service provider did not obtain permission from the authorized organizations for collective management of copyright and related rights;
- the media service provider transferred the concession to another person contrary to the provisions of the EMA;
- the media service provider relayed a permission to another person contrary to the provisions of the EMA;
- the media service provider, despite the decision of the EMC on the measures to temporarily restrict the freedom of transmission of audiovisual media services from other countries, publishes audiovisual programmes under Article 77 of the EMA.[452]

431. The EMC may take appropriate measures to temporarily restrict the freedom of transmission of audiovisual media services from other countries when the Republic of Croatia is authorized to temporarily deviate from the obligation to ensure freedom of reception of audiovisual media services and retransmission on its territory. These measures will be undertaken in relation to the audiovisual media services if:

452. Article 76(1) of the EMA.

- television broadcasts stemming from another Member State of the EU clearly, seriously and severely impair the physical, mental or moral development of minors and/or television broadcasting promotes hatred based on race, sex, religion or nationality;
- in the last twelve months, a television broadcaster acted at least twice according to the preceding subparagraph;
- Croatia has written to inform the television broadcasters and the European Commission on the alleged violations of this Article and the measures to be taken if there are repeated violations;
- consultation with the Member State of the EU carrying out the transfer and the European Commission have not contributed to a friendly settlement within fifteen days of the notification referred to in the preceding subparagraph, and the above violations continue.

432. These measures will be undertaken in relation to the audiovisual media services on request if the following conditions exist:

- if the measures are required for one of the following reasons: public policy, in particular, the prevention, investigation, detection and prosecution of criminal offences, including the protection of minors and the fight against any incitement to hatred based on race, sex, religion or nationality and violations of human dignity of the individual; protection of public health; public security, including the protection of national security and defence as well as the protection of consumers including investors;
- if the Republic of Croatia, before taking the underlying measures, without prejudice to court proceedings, including preliminary proceedings and acts carried out in the framework of a criminal investigation, requested from a Member State, within whose jurisdiction the media service falls, to take measures that the Member State in question did not take or did not take in an appropriate manner;
- the Republic of Croatia has informed the European Commission and the Member State within whose jurisdiction the media service provider falls, of its intent to take action.[453]

433. Finally, it is important to note that the EMC has the authority to submit accusatory motions in order to launch infringement procedures against legal entities and individuals. A fine of HRK 100,000–HRK 1,000,000 shall be imposed on a legal person who:

- carries out activities to provide audio or audiovisual media services and the provision of services of electronic publications and is not entered in the court or other prescribed register as a media service provider or a provider of electronic publications, and does not comply with other conditions of the EMA;
- publishes audio and/or audiovisual media services that threaten the constitutional order and national security;

453. Article 77 of the EMA.

- does not publish free of charge at the request of the competent State authorities the necessary information in case of war or immediate threat to the independence and unity of the Republic of Croatia, as well as in times of natural disasters, technological and environmental disasters and epidemics;
- broadcasts audiovisual commercial communications contrary to the relevant provisions of the EMA;
- broadcasts sponsored audiovisual media services and programmes contrary to the relevant provisions of the EMA;
- broadcasts product placement contrary to the relevant provisions of the EMA;
- carries out activities to provide audio and/or audiovisual media services on-demand opposite to the issued permit;
- transfers permission to another person contrary to the provisions of Article 19, paragraph 7 of the EMA;
- provides audiovisual media services on-demand that may seriously harm the physical, mental or moral development of minors;
- changes or supplements the programme basis for more than 10% of its content contrary to Article 23, paragraph 5 of the EMA;
- broadcasts programmes that offend human dignity, especially immoral and pornographic content, which in any way encourage, promote and glorify violence and crime, and encourage citizens, especially children and youth, to use tobacco, alcohol or drugs;
- broadcasts comparative advertising which is not in accordance with the provisions of the Illegal Advertising Act;
- broadcasts advertising and teleshopping which are not recognized and which are not clearly distinguished from editorial content, or which do not take into account the interests of minors;
- broadcasts advertising and teleshopping of weapons, ammunition and pyrotechnic devices, tobacco and tobacco products and drugs, and alcoholic beverages;
- broadcasts advertising and teleshopping for more than twelve minutes;
- broadcasts programmes sponsored by a political party and coalition, except during election campaign;
- does not perform the obligation of the prescribed share of own production, which is at least 20% of daily broadcasting of each audiovisual programme of the broadcaster of which at least 50% should take place between sixteen and twenty-two hours, or at least 30% of the daily broadcasting time of each radio programme.

Each television broadcaster should strive to comprise the major part of his annual time of publication from European content, and television broadcaster that does not achieve the stated amount of European content must annually increase the proportion of such content in relation to the previous year in accordance with the criteria and manner specified in the Ordinance adopted by the EMC, taking account of the obligations in terms of the informative, educational, cultural and entertainment character of such content:

- if the broadcaster does not achieve the stated ratios, he will be charged with a misdemeanour;

- if the broadcaster does not achieve the minimum share of audiovisual works of independent producers;
- if the broadcaster does not provide the right to short information;
- if the broadcaster links television and radio programmes in the network contrary to the provisions of the EMA;
- if the broadcaster does not publish the share of their own production prescribed for the media service provider of non-profit television and/or radio or publishes advertising messages for more than the time prescribed by the EMA;
- if the broadcaster does not perform the obligation to submit data concerning the shareholders and their shares after a warning from the EMC or does not submit certified copies of documents on the acquisition of shares or units in a media service provider;
- if the broadcaster hides the ownership structure of the media service provider and ownership of the acquirer of shares or units in a media service provider;
- if the broadcaster establishes undue concentration;
- if the broadcaster does not report a change in ownership structure;
- if the broadcaster transfers the concession to another person contrary to the provisions of the EMA;
- if the broadcaster carries out satellite, Internet, cable and other forms of transmission of audiovisual and/or radio programmes without authorization or contrary to the issued permit.[454]

434. For these offences the responsible person in the legal entity shall be fined an amount of HRK 10,000–HRK 50,000. If these offences are committed by a natural person who is a craftsman or a sole trader, they shall be fined an amount of HRK 20,000–HRK 100,000. If any of these violations are committed by a natural person they shall be fined an amount of HRK 10,000–HRK 50,000. Proceeds resulting from an offence shall be forfeited.[455]

435. A fine in the amount of HRK 10,000–HRK 100,000 shall be imposed on a legal person who:

- broadcasts audiovisual or radio programme containing prize competitions which do not fulfil the requirements laid out in the EMA;
- broadcasts sponsored audiovisual media services and programmes which do not fulfil the conditions laid out in the EMA;
- does not mark the rerun of radio or television programmes and/or does not highlight reruns of radio or television programmes in the prescribed manner;
- uses profits from activities contrary to the provisions of the EMA;
- participates in the process of giving concessions contrary to the provisions of the EMA;

---

454. Article 82(1) of the EMA.
455. *Ibid.*

- becomes a television and/or radio broadcaster and/or television and/or radio broadcaster founder, or acquires more than 10% ownership of shares or units, control or voting rights in the capital of a television and/or radio broadcaster contrary to the provisions of the EMA;
- does not perform the obligation of filing the application for registration in the register of the service providers of electronic publications.[456]

436. For these offences, the responsible person in the legal entity shall be fined an amount of HRK 5,000 to HRK 20,000. If these offences are committed by a natural person who is a craftsman or a sole trader, they shall be fined an amount of HRK 10,000 to HRK 50,000. If these offences are committed by a natural person, the person shall be fined an amount of HRK 5,000 to HRK 40,000.[457]

437. The items produced by the perpetration of those offences shall be confiscated and destroyed, and the items that are intended or used for the commission of the referred offences will be confiscated by the State. A legal person, a natural person (either in general, or a craftsman/sole trader), who committed these offences in the performance of their activities may be sanctioned with the suspension of their activities or parts of their activities for up to one year if the infringement is considered particularly offensive because of its manner of execution, the consequences of the acts, the repeated character or any other circumstance which make it particularly offensive. The proceeds resulting from the offence shall be forfeited.

456. Article 83 of the EMA.
457. *Ibid.*

Selected Bibliography

Access to Information Act 2003, Official Gazette No. 172/2003, 144/2010, 37/2011, 77/2011.

Access to Information Act 2013, Official Gazette No. 25/2013.

Act on election of Members of *Sabor*, Official Gazette No. 116/99, 109/00, 53/03, 69/03, 167/03, 44/06, 19/07, 20/09, 145/10, 24/11, 93/11, 120/11, 19/15.

Act on the Government of the Republic of Croatia, Official Gazette No. 150/11, 119/14, 93/16.

Act on craft business, Official Gazette No. 143/13.

Act on salaries in public service, Official Gazette No. 27/01, 39/09.

Administrative Disputes Act, Official Gazette No. 20/10, 143/12, 152/14, 94/16, 29/17.

Alaburić, Vesna, Sloboda misli, mišljenja, izražavanja i informiranja, [Freedom of Thought, Expression and Information], Hrvatska pravna revija [Croatian Law Review] 3(2003) 6, pp. 1–7.

Analogue to Digital Television Broadcasting Switchover Strategy for the Republic of Croatia, July 2008.

Civil Obligations Act, Official Gazette No. 35/05, 41/08, 125/11, 78/15.

Civil Procedure Act Official Gazette No. 53/91, 91/92, 58/93, 112/99, 88/01, 117/03, 88/05, 02/07, 84/08, 123/08, 57/11, 148/11, 25/13, 89/14.

Civil Service Job Titles and Job Complexity Coefficients Regulation Official Gazette [OG] No. 25/13, 72/13,151/13, 09/14, 40/14, 51/14, 77/14, 83/14 – Correction 87/14, 120/14, 147/14, 151/14, 11/15, 32/15, 38/15, 60/15, 83/15, 112/15, 122/15, 10/17, 39/17, 40/17 – Correction, 74/17, 122/17).

Code of Honour of the Croatian Journalists.

Competition Protection Act, Official Gazette No. 79/09, 80/13.

Concessions Act, Official Gazette No. 66/2017.

Courts Act, Official Gazette No. 28/13, 33/15, 82/15, 82/16.

Criminal Code, Official Gazette No. 125/11, 144/12, 56/15, 61/15, 101/17.

Criminal Procedure Code, Official Gazette No. 152/08, 76/09, 80/11, 91/12, 143/12, 56/13, 145/13, 152/14, 70/17.

Croatia in numbers, study of the Croatian Statistics Bureau.

Croatian National Bank Act, Official Gazette No. 75/08, 54/13.

Croatian Radio-Television Act, Official Gazette No. 28/1990.

Croatian Radio-Television Act, Official Gazette No. 137/10, 76/12, 78/16.

Decision of the Constitutional Court No. U-I-241/2000 of 10 May 2000.

Decision of the Constitutional Court No. U-I-274/1996 of 10 July 1996.

Selected Bibliography

Decision on the basis for salaries in public service, Official Gazette OG No. 87/2017.

Electronic Communications Act, Official Gazette No. 73/08, 90/11, 133/12, 80/13, 71/14, 72/17.

Electronic Media Act, Official Gazette No. 153/09, 84/11, 94/13, 136/13.

Electronic Media Agency, TV Market Analysis.

Electronic publication market analysis, HAKOM.

Fabijanić Gagro, S., Vukas, B., *Pravna priroda i politička pozadina oružanih sukoba u Hrvatskoj i Bosni i Hercegovini* [Legal Nature and Political Background of Armed Conflicts in Croatia and Bosnia and Herzegovina], *Zbornik Pravnog fakulteta Sveučilišta u Zagrebu* [University of Zagreb Law School Collected Papers] 58(5) 1159–2000 (2008).

Food Act, Official Gazette No. 81/2013, 14/2014, 30/2015.

HAKOM Broadband Market Analysis.

HAKOM Report for Q3 2017.

HRT's Business and Development Strategy 2013–2017.

HURA – The Croatian Association of Communications Agencies www.hura.hr.

Impermissible Advertising Act, Official Gazette No. 43/2009.

Koprić, I. & Musa, A., What Kind of Agencification in Croatia? Trends and Future Directions, Transylvanian Review of Administrative Sciences, Special Issue 2011.

List of Major Events of the Electronic Media Council.

Ljubić, Dubravko, Ustavna zaštita prava na slobodu misli i izražavanja mišljenja [Constitutional Protection of the Right to Freedom of Thought and Expression], Hrvatska pravna revija [Croatian Law Review], 14 (2014) 11.

Media Act, Official Gazette No. 59/04, 84/11, 81/13.

Medicinal Products Act, Official Gazette No. 76/2013.

Medicines Act, Official Gazette No. 76/2013, 90/2014.

Misdemeanour Act, Official Gazette No. 107/07, 39/13, 157/13, 110/15, 70/17.

Musa, A., Agencies in Croatia: Something Old or Something New? HKJU – CCPA, (2013) No. 2.

Ombudsman for Children Act, Official Gazette No. 73/17.

Ombudsman for Persons with Disabilities Act, Official Gazette No. 107/2007.

Ordinance on Croatian audiovisual works, Official Gazette No. 43/2010.

Ordinance on detailed measures for determining audiovisual and/or radio programmes that are considered in-house productions, Official Gazette No. 132/2014.

Ordinance on minimum standards for conducting audio and audiovisual media services and maintaining the register, Official Gazette No. 83/2014.

Ordinance on minimum standards for conducting audio and audiovisual media services and maintaining the register, Official Gazette No. 83/2014.

Ordinance on the content and procedure of the notice of intent on granting concessions for the provision of television and radio media services, Official Gazette No. 131/2013.

Ordinance on the criteria and manner of increasing the share of the European works, Official Gazette No. 77/2015.

Ordinance on the criteria and manner of increasing the share of the European audiovisual works of independent producers, Official Gazette No. 153/2009, 84/2011, 94/2013 and 136/2013.
Ordinance on the protection of minors in electronic media, Official Gazette No. 28/2015.
Ordinance on the protection of minors in electronic media, Official Gazette No. 28/2015.
Ordinance on the register of providers of media services, electronic publications and producers of non-profit audiovisual and/or radio programmes, Official Gazette No. 134/2013, 79/2014.
Ordinance on work of Ethical Council of the CJA.
Personal Information Protection, Official Gazette No. 103/03, 118/06, 41/08, 130/11, 106/12.
Radio Market Analysis, Ipsos Connect.
Rajko, Alen, Domašaj ustavne odredbe o zabrani cenzure [Reach of the Constitutional Norm on the Prohibition of Censorship], Hrvatska pravna revija [Croatian Law Review], 8 (2008), No. 12.
Rules for the exercise of the right to correction in programmes of audio and audiovisual media service providers, Official Gazette No. 46/2010.
Rules of Procedure of *Sabor*, Official Gazette No. 81/13.
Reuters Institute for the study of Journalism Digital News Report 2017, http://po.st/lfJFXh (23 December 2017).
Smerdel, Branko; Sokol, Smiljko; Ustavno pravo [Constitutional Law], 2009.
Staničić, F., Current Questions of Framework and Action of Regulatory Agencies in the Republic of Croatia [Aktualna pitanja ustroja i djelovanja regulatornih agencija u Republici Hrvatskoj], The Fourth Skopje-Zagreb Colloquium [Četvrti skopsko-zagrebački kolokvij], Skoplje 2013.
State Attorney's Act, Official Gazette No. 76/09, 153/09, 116/10, 145/10, 57/11, 130/11, 72/13, 148/13, 33/15, 82/15.
Statute of Croatian Radio-Television, December 2012.
The Constitution of the Republic of Croatia, Official Gazette No. 56/90, 135/97, 8/98, 113/00, 124/00, 28/01, 41/01, 55/01, 76/10, 85/10, 05/14.
The Contract between Croatian Radio-Television and Government of Republic of Croatia for the period 2013–2017.
The Election of Members to the Croatian Parliament Act, Official Gazette (OG) No. 116/99, 109/00, 53/03, 69/03, 167/03, 44/06, 19/07, 20/09, 145/10, 24/11, 93/11, 120/11, 19/15, 104/15.
The Gender Equality Act, Official Gazette No. 82/08, 69/17.
The Local Elections Act, Official Gazette (OG) No. 114/12, 121/16.

Selected Bibliography

Index

The numbers here refer to the paragraph numbers.

Index

Made in the USA
Monee, IL
18 October 2026

66041416R10090